A New Look at Spiritual Life

A NEW LOOK AT

Spiritual Life

Franklin Atkinson

BROADMAN PRESS
Nashville, Tennessee

Unless otherwise indicated Scripture quotations are from the King James Version of the Bible. Quotations marked (ASV) are from the American Standard Version of the Bible. Quotations marked (NASB) are from the *New American Standard Bible.* Copyright The Lockman Foundation, 1960, 1962, 1963, 1968, 1971, 1972, 1973, 1975, 1977. Used by permission. Quotations marked (RSV) are from the Revised Standard Version of the Bible, copyrighted 1946, 1952, © 1971, 1973.

Library of Congress Cataloging-in-Publication Data

Atkinson, Franklin, 1930-
A new look at spiritual life.

1. Bible. O.T. Malachi—Criticism, interpretation, etc. 2. Spiritual life—Biblical teaching. I. Title.
BS1675.2.A88   1987   224'.9906   86-28325
ISBN 0-8054-1235-2 (pbk.)

Dedicated
to our children

Ruth - Billy   Jean - Mike   David
&   &
Natalie   Jonathan
              Stephanie

Preface

May these studies enrich your spiritual life as they stimulate interest in the revelation of our God committed to Malachi.

Maximum benefit will accrue if the biblical passage is kept in reference as one studies each chapter. An open Bible will enhance one's study.

Acknowledgments

To my wife Barbara, my parents-in-law Mother
 and Dad Harris, and my sisters Evelyn and
 Maudine for encouragement to produce this
 study.
To friends who helped with manuscript editing:
 Ann Bogue, Florine Dean, Carolyn Snow,
 Donald Potts, and Doris and Clarence Williams.

Contents

1
A New Look
at Life's Situation

As the steady dripping of water can cut away a giant rock, so do the little tensors affect our normal ambitions. A huge rocket is made with both highly technical parts and common material. Likewise, life consists of major events and minor details. Decisive decisions merge with day-by-day qualities to determine life's direction. Let us take note of each as we cruise life's course: the rapids and the still waters. A new look may be a fresh look at common elements of life.

Complications within ourselves often include some questions about God, understanding responses to Him, struggles in homemaking, "glass houses" of leadership, and deciding accurately right and wrong. In a reflective stance, Malachi triggers our consideration of many basic human concerns. The book reports the prophet's evaluation of people's complaints. Basic issues remain surprisingly contemporary; so today's preachers find resources for meeting current attitudes in Malachi's message.

Prophetic Worth

The last need not be the least. Size can no longer indicate degrees of power. Lack of familiarity is pitiful measurement of value. Thus, the short book which closes the divine revelation of the Old Testament era beckons us to invest in a new look.

Understandably, the prophet Malachi would need something distinctive to earn a place among the Hebrew greats. He preached during the demise and, therefore, the least exciting period of Israel's history. No ready-made commendation awaited him. The golden age of prophecy—the wonderful eighth century of Amos, Hosea, Isaiah, and Micah—had passed. No favorite seasonal quotations (for example, Christmas) would keep Malachi before the congregation. A new look, therefore, may be necessary to raise people's attention toward his work.

Strategic insights place Malachi with the prophetic giants. His concepts about divine love, the universalism of God's kingdom, and the relation of conduct to divine character propel him into the golden prophetic stream for consideration. Some scholars even doubt his authorship during such bankrupt spiritual and social conditions.

His distinctive style certainly merits the top

grade. He did not possess the vocabulary of Isaiah, the oratory of Amos, the pathos of Hosea, nor the logic of Micah. But Malachi's teaching method is found in the distinctive style of the famous Greek philosopher Socrates. Thus, Malachi is called "the Hebrew Socrates." Some scholars credit him with being the "forerunner of Scholastic Rabbinism."[1] His didactic alteration of Socrates' method of question/answer involved a declaration followed by the audience's objection in the form of a question. The prophetic reply to that question explained the original charge.

Malachi's contribution to succeeding generations of Jewish and, consequently, Christian teaching methods need not be exaggerated. No direct proof can be given of cause and effect. However, during the fifth century BC, the synagogue arose as the center of instruction. Ezra deserves credit for much of that emphasis. Also, we want to honor Malachi for an advancement in style.

Notice evaluations about Malachi's approach. "The dialogue technique made postexilic Hebrew education quite progressive by the standards of earlier centuries."[2] Hailey credits Malachi as being a major contributor to the later educational system: "In the style of Malachi we have the beginning of a method of teaching that later became universal in the Jewish schools and in the synagogue."[3] Observe also F. W. Farrar's estimate: "It is pure and polished but essentially prosaic, and it introduces the new literary machinery of repeated question and answer, a dialectic form of writing which is not without a certain charm of its own, but which opened such facilities for imitation that it became very frequent in the literature of later Judaism."[4]

Dealing with Discouragement

"Then the people of the land weakened the hands of the people of Judah, and troubled them in building" (Ezra 4:4). The *New American Standard Bible* translates this "discouraged" and "frightened."

Discouragement of Being a Little Group

Feelings of inferiority plague many individuals and groups. We claim to be "the best, not the biggest," but secret hurts persist when we are not first or biggest. Comparisons sap energy. That neighboring church's progress, that same-age friend's advancement, and those others' obvious successes sting us. It is easier to "weep with those who weep" than to "rejoice with those who rejoice" because they have more or better.

The Babylonian captivity serves as a major peak of Israel's history alongside Abraham and David (Matt. 1:17). The capital *E* Exile of historians refers to Babylonian, not the Assyrian, captivity. The ending of nationhood, the plundering of their political capital, and the demolishing of their magnificient religious Temple crushed the spirit of the Jews. Read the Book of Lamentations for a feel of their despair.

But God did not die in 586 BC. He remained with the captives, giving sweet assurances (Ezek. 1). He prospered them, thrusting some into governmental positions, really a remarkable feat for refugees (Dan. 1:19; 6:2; Esther 2:17; Neh. 1:11). He arranged for sympathetic foreign rulers to reestablish the Judean homeland and even to help finance the project (Isa. 45:1-7; Ezra 1:1-4; Neh. 2:8).

Yet, like us, they struggled with the sense of loss—remembering when they had been bigger, probably better. Although they could console themselves with the reality of changing conditions (economic and social), they confronted the stories of their glorious past. It stung. They must have assured themselves of being in God's will currently, and they must have enjoyed His presence. That fact should thrill and satisfy. But, rather, some reflected on abounding evidence of divine prosperity because of greater influence and affluence during the Kingdom days. Now they had no king, only a governor; they remained a Persian state.

The group was small and weak. What could the preacher do to instill hope and ambition, even self-

respect? How can our small churches maintain
confidence amidst the barrage of achievements by
"supersized" churches?

Several examples teach us that size is no true
measure of power. Consider the atom, the twelve
disciples, the 120 pray-ers at Pentecost, the two or
three in Jesus' name (character, authority), and
spiritually powered little David.

Motivation can, of course, propel little ones into
major victories. Dependability showed its strength
in the following football record. In November,
1899, the University of the South (Sewanee, TN)
team launched a terrific road trip by defeating
powerful and unbeaten Texas University 12-0. The
next day they smashed Texas A & M 32-0 and then
shut out a talented Tulane team 23-0. The players
rested on Sunday. But on November 12th, Sewanee continued its winning ways by downing a
strong Louisiana State squad 34-0. The 12-0 victory
over Mississippi State closed the trip the next day.
Thus in six days Sewanee played five games,
racked up 113 points against none for five oppo-
nents, traveled 3,000 miles with difficult transpor-
tation (as compared to ours). Now hold your hat:
the team had only 12 players and represented a
student body of 97 men! Determination and dependability win without looking for substitutes.

Discouragement of Roller-Coaster Response to Resolutions

Some people quit rededicating their lives because of their own broken promises. They are sincere, they try, but they fall. So many individuals pace the aisles so frequently that questions are raised about their determination to improve. How can the preacher inspire yet another attempt?

Imagine the thrill capturing the people when they learned about Cyrus's decree that they could go to Judah (536 BC). But many chose to stay in their established homes of Babylon and Persia. Those who traveled found adventure stimulating. They possessed a wonderfully sweet spirit of oneness (Ezra 3:1). They engaged their religious commitment seriously by setting up their altar (v. 3). They were terrified by enemies and clung to their devotion (v. 3). They worshiped by sacrifices and free-will financial offerings. They constructed the foundation of the new Temple (v. 10). Religious fervor swept the congregation like that of a suburban mission. Rejoicing dominated their gatherings (v. 11). Yet some wept, remembering more glorious days of the original Solomon's Temple (vv. 12-13).

How long does enthusiasm last in this earthly environment? How far will excitement carry the group? How much will the desire of God matter? Trouble spilled upon them. Criticism and aggravation disturbed them. Consequently, "Then ceased the work of the house of God which is at Jerusalem." And it remained stopped for fourteen years (Ezra 4:24). Imagine the emotional extremes, the highs and the lows. Think about the resultant drain, even exhaustion.

However, revival days appeared across the bleak horizon. Haggai challenged them to check up (Hag. 1:5) on the real cause of failure. They, as we do today, blamed time and finances instead of self-interests (vv. 2-4). Haggai demanded that they face up (v. 7) to the reality of false prosperity (vv. 6-11). The thrilling response caused them to shape up (vv. 12-14) and to enjoy the "I am with you, saith the Lord." They completed the new Temple in 516 BC.

How often does a building program have a reverse effect? Instead of continued growth of attendance, it may remain the same, causing discouragement. People sometimes assume that buildings will attract new people; but buildings cannot visit, smile, welcome, teach, or meet personality hungers. Sometimes emotional stress during construction produces exhaustion. Prospect files may become weak and lean because of diverted effort during the building process. Leadership may change. The flames of building enthusiasm may give way to only smoke.

How long do revivals last on a national impact

scale? Ezra found out. Fifty-eight years later (458 BC) he led another group from Babylon. He found a disappointing situation. People had drifted from religious devotion. They carelessly kept the Mosaic law. They had wandered from marriage loyalties. Spiritual leadership had waned from the quality of Haggai and Zechariah. Indifference gripped the population. They needed spiritual awakening. Ezra, the priest and scribe, called the citizens to prayer, to the Word of God, and to repentance (Ezra 9—10).

But despondency persisted. Nehemiah in Persia spoke with a delegation who reported that the group was "in great affliction and reproach" (Neh. 1:3). Therefore, he sat down and cried. The date was about 444 BC. The lack of a city wall provoked their depression of spirit. Nehemiah's countenance reflected his disturbance. His employer, the king, sent Nehemiah to direct the reconstruction of a wall.

This dedicated layman challenged associates that it was a "great work" (6:3). They caught Nehemiah's enthusiasm and thus worked and fought to complete the project because "the people had a mind to work" (4:6). Dedication events expressed their delight (12:27).

But much teaching, confession, and covenanting remained to be done. See Nehemiah 8—10. Skepticism mixed with apathy produces a tough wall. A prophetic voice was needed. Malachi exposed their complaints and errors. A new look reveals how contemporary they are. For the people's eight replies reveal a sophisticated self-righteousness which comforts their consciences. Ideas about sin and repentance belong to the bad guys, not religiously active worshipers! How could a preacher get through that snobish shell?

The Prophet's Name

Scholars debate whether the word *Malachi* is a proper name or a description (see 3:1). Because we know nothing else about a prophet by that name, some doubt that the word should be used as a name.

Also, some interpreters (Targum, Jerome, Rabbi Rashi, Calvin) consider the word to be descriptive of Ezra. But because of the following reasons, we may accept the word to be a personal name: (1) other prophets were unknown (Obadiah), (2) other names were so constructed ("Beeri," "Ethni," "Abi"), and (3) the text projected it comfortably. The meaning is "My Messenger" or "My angel."

Environment

Correct understanding of God's actions and instructions begin with His relation to humanity in specific situations. Thus, to grasp these historical matters should enhance the application of divine truth. Marvelous inspiration can yet reach us even within limited recognition of original circumstances.

The conditions of their society reflect those very similar to the time of Ezra and Nehemiah. Strong priestly functions, decayed religious practices, marriage/divorce, "governor," and the absence of political enemies internationally indicate that the historical period was about 444-432 BC. Bible students would serve themselves well to review Ezra, Nehemiah, and Haggai to sense the urgency of Malachi. To note the eagerness of the first returnees from Babylon to begin the Temple is exciting. To see the loss of it with attention on self-interests is instructive about human behavior.

Zerubbabel and Joshua had led the first group from Babylon in 536 BC. After a fourteen-year lapse of building activity, Haggai and Zechariah stirred the people to complete the new Temple. Ezra took a second group in 458 BC. Nehemiah, in Persia, was saddened because of the despondency of the returnees. He was granted leave from his governmental position to lead in building the city wall which was quite meaningful to people of ancient times. Such encouragement helped.

Malachi preached against that background. Religious and social values remained quite low. We associate with people who will face some of these crisis situations. Our churches will match in many

ways the people of God in Malachi's day. May our
God enlighten us in profitable application of this
prophet's challenges.

God's Word

The little book contains fifty-five verses. Forty-
seven are first-person addresses from Yahweh.
"This use of the first person presents a vivid encounter between God and the people, unsurpassed
in the prophetic books."[5] Such style magnifies the
value of the Old Testament's last voice.

Notes

1. Thomas J. Delaughter, *Malachi: Messenger of Divine Love* (New Orleans: Insight Press, Inc., 1976), p. 25.
2. Kenneth O. Grangel and Warren S. Benson, *Christian Education: Its
History and Philosophy* (Chicago: Moody Press, 1983), p. 31. Used by permission of Moody Bible Institute of Chicago.
3. Homer Hailey, *A Commentary on the Minor Prophets* (Grand Rapids:
Baker Book House, 1972), p. 402.
4. F. W. Farrar, *The Lives and Times of the Minor Prophets* (London:
James Nisbet and Co., n.d.), p. 225.
5. Joyce G. Baldwin, *Haggai, Zechariah, Malachi* (Downers Grove, Ill.:
Inter-Varsity Press, 1972), p. 216.

2
A New Look
at Love
Malachi 1:2-5

Frequently used terms often become bland, losing the power of their meaning. In our contemporary society the word *love* is pitched rather carelessly toward the winds.

Love Defined

Human frailty distorts our comprehension of divine love. Also, human misconception of any love (human or divine) warps understanding of divine love. In our contemporary society, psychology studies various kinds of abuse: child, mate, and impersonal. One basic conclusion surfaces: love needs to be expressed in homes between mates and constantly to children. Children need to realize love and acceptance, even with or beyond conduct correction. For those who do not experience love tend to be incapable of receiving or giving it later; love is thus a foreign concept to them. Abusers were often the abused ones earlier, growing up in fami-

lies in which violence was an expected normal way
of life.

Consequently, we have difficulty communicat-
ing God's supreme love to our loveless society.
Horrible reports of child molestation abound,
much like heathen practices of child sacrifice by
fire, drowning, or as animal food. National centers
for abuse reporting and therapy are busy.

How can Christians describe convincingly God's
great love to such a society? Perhaps open, honest
exhibition of love comparable to God's love is the
best vehicle. Two basic elements are evident in
real love: unselfishness and desire for positive good
for another.

In a prominent eastern university, a sociology
class surveyed living conditions of an exceptionally
deprived area. They made forecasts of expectations for the children. Most of them should be
criminals and parasites on society. The sociology
department conducted a similar survey of those
persons years later. They were able, surprisingly,
to locate a big majority of those previously recorded. Likewise, surprisingly, the reports indicated
that the vast number of them had no law entanglements and were educated and successfully employed, contributing to their world. While seeking
explanations for the unpredictable result, they ob-
served that in the questioning process, a woman's
name often arose from the individuals. When she

was found and asked what she had done for the people, she was also surprised. She had not been able to fund their leaving the area, nor pay for education. She had naturally loved, accepted, and encouraged them to be their best. The power of love produced ambitious lives.

In order to impress oneself with any degree of comprehending God's love, consider a few human examples of superior, selfless sacrifice. Someone may dash into a flaming building to rescue a loved one. Relatives have offered themselves as substitutes for hostages in dangerous situations. So did Oliver Powers in 1960. His son Francis was the pilot of a U-2 plane on an intelligence mission which was shot down by the Russians. Soviet officials claimed that the pilot would be tried for spying. The father offered himself in exchange saying, "I'm willing to be shot if it will get him home." The great king David wept and declared, "O my son Absalom, my son, my son Absalom! would God I had died for thee, O Absalom, my son, my son!" (2 Sam. 18:33). The strength of love acts.

Likewise, note these biblical illustrations of divine love surpassing extremely strong human love. Even if a mother's love fails, God declares that His care will last (Isa. 49:15). If a man survives the wounded love of his wife's adulterous practices (maybe prostitution-slavery), he is recognized as being far beyond normal human expectations to take her back as God does us (Hos. 1—3). Whereas people may reward good deeds, few would extend themselves to those who do bad, but "God commendeth his love toward us, in that, while we were yet sinners, Christ died for us" (Rom. 5:7-8).

Attempts to define love lead toward describing its action. Combined with unselfishness on one end is the desire for good to the object of love on the other end. James equated one's religious commitment (faith) with love in action by giving to fill needs (Jas. 2:15-16).

One of earth's most sublime expressions of love came from a woman who conquered what would have been normal hurt and hate. Her true story, written by Bob Considine, is quoted from *Guideposts* magazine.

This is the story of a woman's love for her husband. Whether he deserved that love—and why he acted the way he did—are questions I can't answer. I'm not going to write about Karl Taylor; this story is about his wife.

The story begins early in 1950 in the Taylors' small apartment in Waltham, Massachusetts. Edith Taylor was sure that she was "the luckiest woman on the block." She and Karl had been married 23 years, and her heart still skipped a beat when he walked into the room.

As for Karl, he gave every appearance of a man in love with his wife. Indeed, he seemed almost dependent on her, as if he didn't want to be too long away from her. If his job as government warehouse worker took him out of town, he'd write Edith a long letter every night and drop her postcards several times during the day. He sent small gifts from every place he visited.

Often at night they'd sit up late in their apartment and talk about the house they'd own, someday, "when we can make the down-payment. . . ."

In February, 1950, the government sent Karl to Okinawa for a few months to work in a new warehouse. It was a long time to be away, and so far!

This time, no little gifts came. Edith understood. He was putting every cent he saved into the bank for their home. Hadn't she begged him for years not to spend so much on her, to save it for the house?

The lonesome months dragged on, and it seemed to Edith that the job over there was taking longer and longer. Each time she expected him home he'd write that he must stay "another three weeks." "Another month." "Just two months longer."

He'd been gone a year now—and suddenly Edith had an inspiration. Why not buy their home now, before Karl got back, as a surprise for him! She was working now, in a factory in Waltham, and putting all her earnings in the bank. So she made a down-payment on a cozy cottage with lots of trees and a view.

Karl's letters were coming less and less often. No gifts she understood. But a few pennies for a postage stamp?

Then, after weeks of silence, came a letter:

"Dear Edith. I wish there were a kinder way to tell you that we are no longer married. . . ."

Edith walked to the sofa and sat down. He'd written to Mexico for a divorce. It had come in the mail. The woman lived on Okinawa. She was Japanese; Aiko, maid-of-all-work assigned to his quarters.

She was 19. Edith was 48.

Now, if I were making up this story, the rejected wife would feel first shock, then fury. She would fight that quick paper-divorce, she would hate her husband and the woman. She would want vengeance for her own shattered life.

But I am describing here simply what did happen. Edith Taylor did not hate Karl. Perhaps she had loved him so long she was unable to stop loving him.

She could picture the situation so well. A penniless girl. A lonely man who—Edith knew it—sometimes drank more than he should. Constant closeness. But even so (here Edith made an heroic effort to be proud of her husband)—even so, Karl had not done the easy, shameful thing. He had chosen the hard way of divorce, rather than take advantage of a young servant-girl.

The only thing Edith could not believe was that he had stopped loving her. That he loved Aiko, too, she made herself accept.

But the difference in their ages, in their backgrounds —this couldn't be the kind of love she and Karl had known! Someday they would both discover this—someday, somehow, Karl would come home.

Edith now built her life around this thought. She wrote Karl, asking him to keep her in touch with the small, day-to-day things in his life. She sold the little cottage with its view and its snug insulation. Karl never knew about it.

He wrote one day that he and Aiko were expecting a baby. Marie was born in 1951, then in 1953, Helen. Edith sent gifts to the little girls. She still wrote to Karl and he wrote back, the comfortable, detailed letters of two people who knew each other very well: Helen had a tooth, Aiko's English was improving, Karl had lost weight.

Edith's life was lived now on Okinawa. She merely went through the motions of existence in Waltham. Back and forth between factory and apartment, her mind was always on Karl. Someday he'll come back. . . .

And then the terrible letter: Karl was dying of lung cancer.

Karl's last letters were filled with fear. Not for himself, but for Aiko, and especially for his two little girls. He had been saving to send them to school in America, but his hospital bills were taking everything. What would become of them?

Then Edith knew that her last gift to Karl could be peace of mind for these final weeks. She wrote him that, if Aiko were willing, she would take Marie and Helen and bring them up in Waltham.

For many months after Karl's death, Aiko would not let the children go. They were all she had ever known. Yet what could she offer them except a life like hers had been? A life of poverty, servitude and of despair. In

November, 1956, she sent them to her "Dear Aunt Edith."

Edith had known it would be hard to be mother at 54 to a three-year-old and a five-year-old. She hadn't known that in the time since Karl's death they would forget the little English they knew.

But Marie and Helen learned fast. The fear left their eyes, their faces grew plump. And Edith—for the first time in six years—was hurrying home from work. Even getting meals was fun again!

Sadder were the times when letters came from Aiko. "Aunt. Tell me now what they do. If Marie or Helen cry or not." In the broken English Edith read the loneliness, and she knew what loneliness was.

Money was another problem. Edith hired a woman to care for the girls while she worked. Being both mother and wage-earner left her thin and tired. In February she became ill, but she kept working because she was afraid to lose a day's pay; at the factory one day she fainted. She was in the hospital two weeks with pneumonia.

There in the hospital bed, she faced the fact that she would be old before the girls were grown. She thought she had done everything that love for Karl asked of her, but now she knew there was one thing more. She must bring the girls' real mother here too.

She had made the decision, but doing it was something else. Aiko was still a Japanese citizen, and that immigration quota had a waiting list many years long.

It was then that Edith Taylor wrote to me, telling me her story and asking if I could help her. I described the situation in my newspaper column. Others did more. Petitions were started, a special bill speeded through Congress and, in August, 1957, Aiko Taylor was permitted to enter the country.

As the plane came in at New York's International Airport, Edith had a moment of fear. What if she should hate this woman who had taken Karl away from her?

The last person off the plane was a girl so thin and small Edith thought at first it was a child. She did not come down the stairs, she only stood there, clutching the railing, and Edith knew that, if she had been afraid, Aiko was near panic.

She called Aiko's name and the girl rushed down the steps and into Edith's arms. In that brief moment, as they held each other, Edith had an extraordinary thought. "Help me to love this girl, as if she were part of Karl, come home. I prayed for him to come back. Now he has—in his two little daughters and in this gentle girl that he loved. Help me, God, to know that."[1]

Seeing the unselfishness of God combined with desire for good to the object, William R. Newell wrote:

> Oh, the love that drew salvation's plan!
> Oh, the grace that bro't it down to man!
> Oh, the mighty gulf that God did span
> At Calvary.

Love Beyond Circumstances—1:2*b*

Real love reaches beyond temporal circumstances. But we are so engulfed in our affairs that we find it difficult to turn our eyes upon Jesus and discover that His glory and grace are sufficient for us.

"Now what is that supposed to mean?" is an expression which often shows a retort by question or implication, perhaps a note of accusation. That is what the people's response was in their question, "Wherein hast thou loved us?" The question was not for a list whereby they could give praises for each item. Rather the question was a response of accusation, for their plight seemed to speak of God's disfavor. The deplorable conditions (described in ch. 1 previously) projected a God-forgotten concept. Consider how things looked from their viewpoint: smallness of size, limited influence, little prestige, and such a dependent status politically on Persia. Surely God was not loving them and permitting that to happen! Or imagine from someone's estimate of God's viewpoint: degenerate spiritual leaders (1:6), apathy to God's will and stated law of acceptable offerings (1:7), regular tithing practice (3:8-9), and interreligious marriages (2:11). Surely God would not keep on loving them!

Popular religion of today emphasizes the

"health and wealth" theology. In some circles, the preaching actually offers material rewards of God's pleasure when we obey. He has stated such care in certain places. However, making the universal application causes us interpretation problems. However, the opposite concept occurs, "You don't love me unless you give me what I want."

But with many of us a more hidden similar expectation operates. Notice our testimonies at Thanksgiving time. We are expressive for "good health, good families, and good comforts." Of course, we must be grateful for luxuries of His grace in the good and perfect gifts from above. But we need to be grateful also for the painful gifts that produced good in us or those left unexplained. We declare evidence of God's favor if conditions are pleasant such as the following situations. "God was really with us Sunday, for we had lots of additions." Or "God was with us because the building construction progressed on schedule." Or "God was pleased with us because things fell into place conveniently as the breadwinner got a job with a good salary, sold the house rather quickly (with profit), and found a lovely house at the new location (at a bargain price)."

The Jews used the references of blessings and success to develop the belief of divine favor with the obtaining of children, long life, and material prosperity. Thus, the experience of Job in such

earthly losses was obvious disfavor in the opinions
of his friends.

Explaining why God sometimes gives those comfortable benefits to us and at other times does not
is beyond us. Martha was perplexed, perhaps even
complaining, when she said to Jesus, "Lord, if thou
hadst been here, my brother had not died" (John
11:21). Elijah had struggles when he did not see
the God of miracles at Mount Carmel take care of
Jezebel's threat to end his life (1 Kings 18—19).
Moreover, the God of deliverance, who led Simon
Peter out of the prison with such graphic miracle,
permitted James to be killed (Acts 12). Perhaps we
do well to let God still be sovereign and worthy of
our trust in His nature of love.

Does our prayer, "Lord, be with . . ." really mean
"Lord, be sure to arrange the outcome like we
desire"? Practical expressions of this show up in
our prayer desiring relief of pain, safety in travel
(no detours or delays), payment of bills, cooperation of children, passing of school courses, and
other pleasant successes.

Subconsciously people often maintain a suspi-
cion that God may not always be good for their
best interest. For some reserve themselves, as if
they dare not say it aloud, wondering: *If I surren-
dered completely to God, would He make me do
something silly or send me to some awful, unreasonable place?*

Which one of us might join those Israelites in the
cynical question implying that God's statement of
His love was hollow platitude or wishful thinking?
The evidence could point to the promise being
incredible in light of the depressing circumstances.
But humanity tends to overlook items that could
have been counted as divine benefits. The Jews
were still a national entity. They had been delivered from Babylonian captivity, although those
who stayed in Babylon might have lived fairly
prosperous lives. They did have a Temple and
seemed to have peaceful relations with other nations.

Children throw at parents this charge of not
being loved, "You don't love me unless you let me
do as I please." Parents reply, "I love you so much
that I am going to do all I can to keep you from
hurting yourself." Children grow beyond parental
control and decisions. Still parents have to face the
"you don't love me" threat. They either keep bail-
ing children out or permit the children to face
their actions either to learn by experiencing the
consequences or by suffering if the consequences
are final. This same argument about God's love
denies His permitting people to go to a place with
conditions like hell. But love allows choice and
decision.

Even disciplinary actions rise from a tough love.
Such love includes correction, even punishment. It

is better than rewarding wrong in people, teaching them to persist in error. Because God loves, He disciplines and punishes. His declaration that "I have loved you" laid the groundwork in Malachi's message for future rebukes and promises. Moreover, love remains even when out of sight as beyond the dark unknown stands God keeping watch over His own.

Love Amidst Righteousness—1:3*b*-4

The impact of this message strikes clearest when viewed as being directed to its target audience— Israel (1:1). God spoke to challenge Israel, not defend His character to Esau (Edomites). The heart of the divine reply is in election love, covenant love, sustaining love, and justice love. The purpose was to gain favorable response of dedication. Consequently, questions of partiality and hatefulness are incidental to the thrust of the problem. However, we shall consider them later.

Reassurance of divine love is stated in the verb *love*. The tense is perfect which means completed action. Hebrew verbs do not have time as does English. The context determines the temporal interpretation. Normally completed action finds easy fulfilment in the past. However, characteristic actions are timeless. Therefore, the verb means that God has loved in the past, does love now in the present, and will continue to love in the future.

That present time aspect disturbed Malachi's audience. Therefore, God triggered their memory about His faithfulness with the illustration about election.

Divine election of the Hebrew family began with Abram, and it continued with the choice of Isaac rather than Ishmael. The situation between Jacob and Esau further exhibited divine projection of purpose. Moses spoke of the national significance when he declared, "The Lord did not set his love upon you, nor choose you, because ye were more in number than any people; for ye were the fewest of all people: but because the Lord loved you, and because he would keep the oath which he had sworn unto your fathers" (Deut. 7:7-8).

The purpose of election sheds light, although not answering all complaints, upon the use of one people rather than another. Basically, service toward others remains the key. When God calls a physician to live among a people, He displays His love for the people, not a selfish honoring of the physician as someone specially loved and pampered. Thus Israel was to give herself for the benefit of the Gentiles from the first covenant: "in thee shall all the families of the earth be blessed" (Gen. 12:3c). The special grammatical form also emphasized that it was demanded: "Be thou a blessing" (Gen. 12:2c, ASV). Space prohibits full listing of such evidence. But note that outreach to non-Hebrew people abounds in their history. At the Temple dedication Solomon prayed, "That all the people of the earth may know that the Lord is God, and that there is none else" (1 Kings 8:60). Election provided opportunity for missionary service rather than for any selfish, special salvation privileges. Note Paul's use of Abram as an example of salvation by grace and his appeal to Genesis 15:6 (Rom. 4:1-3).

Covenant love vouched for divine faithfulness to struggle with weak, perhaps fickle, human instruments. Such dependable commitment was founded upon divine sovereignty as it expressed itself in election. Humanity must permit God to know more than we and to act in accord with His nature of real love for all peoples. Questions about divine dealings persist today as much as in ancient times. For example, do we demand to know why some people are favored to be born in certain environments in contrast to others? Paul expounded on the sovereignty aspect in Romans 9:10-18. Jeremiah stated God's determined care, although He often condemned His people's sinfulness. Jeremiah declared of God, "I have loved thee with an everlasting love: therefore with lovingkindness have I drawn thee" (Jer. 31:3b).

God's sustaining love rises to Malachi's audience. The complaint challenged God's declaration of contemporary care. God's continuing relationship amidst their sin marked a marvelous quality in Him. Worthiness has not been the determining factor, then or now. Would it serve to gain a favorable response from God—then or now?

Let us consider the problems raised by the Jacob/Esau illustration. Two elements plague our sensitivity: partiality and hatefulness. Residents of a democratic government expect to advise (correct) their chief of state. They need to recognize that the sovereign God is not affected by human opinions. Frail humanity has exhibited too many limitations of knowledge and achievements to alter divine choices. Horizons are too narrow for a universal look. Recall also that this message was directed to Israel, not to Edom. God could have exposed evidences of love toward Esau/Edom if required. Esau's line did not worship Yahweh. Therefore, biblical records do not recount divine actions toward them. The interpreter must decide to what extent he is willing to trust divine inspiration and protection of an accurate record of these matters.

Study of the original Jacob/Esau predictions illuminates the picture in Malachi. Esau's spiritual defects are well discussed by Watts. Genesis 25:23 is a prophecy indicating election according to the foreknowledge of God, but it does not mean a mechanical and unrighteous fixing of future events. Esau's despising of his birthright was revelation of his character. God's choice was based on moral and spiritual considerations, not on human customs that the birthright belonged to the oldest son. Watts declared that "there was nothing in him to appeal to, to instruct, and to develop into an inheritance of the blessing." Watts also explained as follows:

When Esau despised his birthright he did despite to the Spirit. He manifested a complete lack of spiritual appreciation. When he tried later to make a distinction between birthright and blessing, when begging his father to bless him despite the blessing already given to Jacob (cf. Gen. 27:36), he manifested spiritual blindness. He speaks of the birthright with the leadership it conferred as something separate from the blessing. Evidently the blessing to him was merely freedom to do as he pleased, combined with prosperity. But such could not be among the people of Yahweh. The whole point is that he completely lacked spiritual understanding of Yahweh, had no faith in Yahweh, and for that he was condemned. So it is with all who are condemned.[2]

Further expression of defiance of Yahweh's will may be seen in Esau's marriage to pagan women (Gen. 26:34-35; 28:8). New Testament evaluation of Esau will be seen in Hebrews 12:16.

Contemporary students have difficulty with hereditary aspects of condemnation. We emphasize personal rights. However, present-day child abuse causes us to see more clearly the contagious influence of the home. That descendants chose similar dispositions may be evident in the Book of Obadiah. Note also Jeremiah 49:7.

How do we understand Yahweh's hatred for Esau? God has been charged with the character defect of unreasonable passion. The term *hate* may be understood to be indicative of a softer meaning than sheer absolute hatred. Admittedly, some scholars insist otherwise. The same Hebrew word in Malachi 1:3 ("hate") is rendered "dislike" or "spurn" in other texts (Deut. 21:15; 22:13,16; 24:3). Likewise, a close parallel is seen in Jacob's view of Rachel and Leah in Genesis 29:30-33. Meanings there are for preference, a ranking. The Hebrew concept and Oriental hyperbole can be used to emphasize a point dramatically. The Jewish flavor of New Testament writings may also illustrate the practice. Note the parallel passages of Matthew 10:37 and Luke 14:26 in which the terms "more than" and "hate" are used interchangeably.

Justice love must express itself. The captivity declared it. The alarm of Israel's future must be sounded (Mal. 1:14, 3:5). Consequently, Malachi's report that Yahweh had acted in Edomite history to express His wrath (1:5) ought to serve as warning to Israel. Probably the reality of territorial devastation was performed by the Nabataean Arabs between 550 BC and 400 BC, perhaps in Malachi's day. Petra was a military fortress considered to be unconquerable. Now forsaken and desolate it screams of lessons that need to be heard. Human pride cannot match the justice of the Almighty. See Obadiah's prediction against Edom. Desolation was determined by Yahweh, although Edom had pride, power, and protection from enemies. Israel and our own citizens should take note.

Love Beyond Borders—1:5

Who would then recognize the marvelous love of God? The prophet proclaimed a doxology as a fitting conclusion of reflection upon divine love. You can appropriate it by meditating upon the various facets of the text.

The doubting audience will have evidence for convincingness if they will receive. Let those who have eyes to see really recognize God's truthfulness. They have opportunity also to expose—to relay—that learned fact. New discoveries sometime thrill people into expressive stimulation such as "Come and see" (John 1:39,46). Thus Malachi said, "Your eyes shall see, and ye shall say. . . ."

The verb in the direct quotation means "to make great, to grow, to magnify." The grammar permits either a declaration or a wish. Either Yahweh will be magnified in the recognition of the audience, or may He be (He should be) magnified. The greatness of God is declared by the prophet because of his faithfulness to covenant love to Israel and His justice love to Edom.

Scholars differ concerning the meaning of "from the border of Israel." Practically equal textual evidence of etymology and contextual interpretation exists. Also, equal quality of scholarship takes differing views. In such cases, many devotional students take both!

One group sees the acknowledgment "beyond the borders" of Israel by other peoples. Thus a missionary thrust is given. As God's activities with the pharaoh of Egypt were to require admission of Yahweh's might, so the Gentiles would correspondingly face it in His dealings with Israel and Edom as described above. Such "beyond the borders" message would also indicate that Yahweh is not a territorial God only of the Jews because He was active in the affairs of Edom. See also Jeremiah 1:5c ("nations") and his chapters 46—51. Quality translations render the text this way (ASV, RSV).

Another group prefers to enjoy the translation "over the borders." The Hebrew word can mean that. Therefore, they rejoice in Yahweh's greatness as a protective canopy of love over Israel as He struggles to win a favorable response.

In either case, Yahweh's answer to the skeptical "wherein" results in praise of His faithfulness to His people as well as His righteousness toward wickedness. The summary serves as a base for continuing preaching for a repentant response. The threatening nature of God's message was expressed in "The burden of the word of the Lord." The reality of His chastening should be recalled from their captivity experience. But also His current presence, expressed by a sent messenger, should refresh their recognition of His steadfast determination to love, to work, and to win His people.

May God be praised "above" the borders of His own, and even "beyond" those borders in every land and by every tribe, tongue, and nation. To Him be all glory forever!

Notes

1. Bob Considine, "Could You Have Loved This Much?" *Guideposts,* Jan. 1966, pp. 4-7. Adapted with permission from Guideposts Magazine. Copyright © 1959 by Guideposts Associates, Inc., Carmel, New York 10512.

2. J. Wash Watts, *Old Testament Teaching* (Nashville: Broadmam Press, 1967), pp. 50,55.

3
A New Look
at Leadership
Malachi 1:6; 2:1-9

"What the world needs is love, sweet love" remains true for all ages, backward as well as forward. The divine declaration: "I have loved you" (Mal. 1:2), provided the basic foundation for relationship and challenge to improve Israel's relationship with God.

Love has power. Examples are given of love bursting barriers, crushing criticism, and building bridges. The goodness of God could lead to repentance (Rom. 4:4). Malachi extended such consideration.

Human response does not always operate logically. The religious leaders had not been attracted to that love; thus we confront another divine reprimand followed by human accusing question (Mal. 1:6).

Responsibility of Choice

The horribleness producing the divine charge presents itself in the "despise my name." To despise is to evaluate with contempt. It measures the worth to be nothing. Obviously, the normal consequence would be to disregard God's wishes, commands, or threats. Furthermore, conduct follows concept. What we consider to be important gets our attention. What we think is worthless or useless we neglect or forget.

To obtain the size of this problem, we must get beyond our Western culture understanding of the word *name*. Such grasp of the Hebrew concept, however, will greatly enhance our interpretation of all those tremendous New Testament passages, for example, "in my name," "by the name," and "in the name of the Father, Son, and Holy Spirit."

Names were given to describe a person, not merely to identify him or her. Our use of "Junior" approximates their use. A distinctive name was given to describe status, like "Abram," meaning "Exalted Father." But, when the status changed, the name changed to "Abraham," meaning "Father of a multitude."

Names were selected to describe a person's character. "Jacob," meaning "supplanter," changed when the character (or nature) changed to "Isra-

el," meaning "striven with God" or "prince of
God" (Gen. 32:27-28).

Names were used to describe accurately events
and places; so "Peniel" revealed that the "face of
God" had been seen (Gen. 32:30). "Bethel" projected an encounter with God as "house of God"
(Gen. 28:16-19).

Names were employed to declare the nature of
a person. The "Jacob"-"Israel" combination could
so indicate. "Sarai" exposed her as "contentious";
whereas "Sarah" means "princess," referring to
her relation with many nations (Gen. 17:15-16).
"Jesus" would save us from our sins (Matt. 1:21) as
that name means "Savior." We thrill at the revelation of Yahweh's nature proclaimed in Exodus 34:
6-7.

Therefore, the wonderfully enriching story of
Yahweh's personal name excites our study. Eve, in
Genesis 4:1, apparently referred to Him as the
Giver of spiritual life since she and Adam had the
basic part in producing Cain's physical body.

Progress in the content of that name *Yahweh*
arose in their experience. The civilization thereaf-
ter was confounded with problems they could not
handle: murder, death, haughtiness, and polyga-
my. Those parents named a child Enos, meaning
weak or mortal. Since Enos lived 905 years (Gen.
5:11), he must have been strong physically. Therefore, his name reflects the morbid fear of death and

such human frailties that they could not fix. In Genesis 5 the recurring reality punctuates the record—'and he died." Consequently, in Genesis 4:26 we discover, ". . . then began men to call upon the name of the Lord." "The Lord" in that verse translates this personal name, "JHWH, Yahweh." People did not merely pronounce it. They depended on the character ("name") of Yahweh to be a helper of life or "Sustainer of life."

The special name would grow in its significance of people's continuing experience to learn different qualities of God. The problem passage becomes clearer when we realize that the Hebrew text has the definite article "the" with "name" (Gen. 6:4). The "same" were "men of the name," not "men of a name," meaning "renown." This literary device would connect them with the saints who called upon the name of Yahweh in Genesis 4—5. The word *Shem* (for our "Semite") means "name." Noah's righteous son was called "name." Noah declared, "Blessed be the Lord God of Shem" to indicate that Shem's character related to the Deity (Gen. 9:26).

Moses, facing an impossible task, wanted to know God's character (name) for the project. His concern was not letters in sequence to identity one person from another (Ex. 3:13). Considering the facts, the "Yahweh" name absorbed additional content of that marvelous new revelation. The words translated "I am that I am" (Ex. 3:14, KJV) are two verbs with a pronoun between them. Hebrew verbs do not contain time. Time comes from the context. The exact word, spelled identically as "I am" of Exodus 3:14, is translated "I will be" in Exodus 3:12 (KJV). The American Standard Version provides a note, which is often overlooked, showing that the name can accurately be translated "I will be." Because the deliverance project was future to the call of Moses, we can use "I will be" for the verbs. Also, because the revelation of God's name (character) was emphasized in the covenant relations of the past (Ex. 3:6), we can translate the verb "I have been." Therefore, a marvelous additional meaning in Moses' experience can arise in an accurate translation of the text combining those two temporal facts, "I will be what I have been." Thus, dependability shines as a character quality for the new, impossible task. And, the name "Yahweh" would absorb this element of faithfulness in Moses' use of that name.

Later the zenith of revelation arrived when God Himself defined that personal name *Yahweh* to include the moral qualities of His nature. In the context of discovering forgiveness for sin (Ex. 32) and in response to Moses' request that God show him His "glory" (essence), God proclaimed that name in moral terms: "The Lord, the Lord God, merciful and gracious, longsuffering, and abundant in goodness and truth, Keeping mercy for thousands, forgiving iniquity and transgression and sin, and that will by no means clear the guilty" (34:5-7). That theological definition of the name (character/nature) remained in the prophetic stream of Israel: Jonah 4:2; Joel 2:13; and Micah 7:18.

That tremendous heritage stimulated early Christians to use the word *name* to refer to the status, character, or nature of Jesus. Thus, to pray in His name means to pray in accord with His character, not merely pronounce His name. Likewise, although often omitted when the passage is quoted, the words "in my name" makes the difference where two or three are gathered expecting His presence (Matt. 18:20).

We, therefore, realize from this history that Malachi's audience was despising the very person of God, not merely a reference title. Such a charge takes on extreme seriousness. Consequently, they would not live to honor or to glorify that God ("name" in 2:2) or to reverence him ("fear" in 2:5).

The challenge remains for us to honor Him, His reputation entrusted to us, and His worship.

Righteous Expectations

With the character qualities of God evident, we can easily accept that His associates in service should desire to be parallel in consecration. Malachi's challenge returned to the leaders—the priests —in chapter 2:1-9.

Covenant privilege motivates the devoted to sincere service (Mal. 2:4). Reference to the covenant with Levi is found in Deuterononmy 18:1-8 and 33:8-11. Nehemiah considered that such a covenant was in their understanding (Neh. 13:29). This statement seems to reflect that call to service. Christian leadership ought to take careful notice in order to be the most that we can be for the Savior.

The urging of the moment with our leaders is intended to be refreshing, an encouragement, and a source for endurance. It could be like the retreats or pastors/evangelism conferences at which we receive stimulus to be better, to last longer. The hope is for authentic openness with self, not a pressure of "glasshouse" expectations. The desire is that in confident reality, not pretending superficiality, the Christian leader enjoy supremely the covenant call. Our divine call compares to the covenant with Levi (Mal. 2:4-5).

Chester Swor laid just such a challenge on the future servants of the Lord at the New Orleans Baptist Theological Seminary. He prepared a questionnaire for laymen since he was delivering the Tharp Lectures with the intention of exposing "The Minister from the Layman's Viewpoint." Ninty-five laymen from twenty different states and thirty-three occupational classifications respond-

ed. A surprisingly large number manifested concern for the spiritual anchorings of their minister.
They wanted no trace of doubt in the minister's
mind about his regeneration conversion. They
desired "that he be genuinely called into the ministry. . . . That he have an overwhelming sense of
mission or 'call.' " Asked to point out the thing
in favorite pastors' lives which had helped and
inspired the laymen most, they accented "dedication," which they usually defined as "unselfishness."

In addition to the covenant of service, Malachi
urged honesty in conduct (v. 6a): "The law of truth
was in his mouth, and iniquity was not found in his
lips." According to Swor's survey, the laymen
unanimously desired, first of all, that the minister's
"character be completely above reproach, and
that he avoid even the appearance of evil in his
behavior." We need not rebel at this as if it is unreasonable criticism or expectation. Laymen are
not demanding sinless attainment, the absolute
avoidance of a "slip." Their explanation of character traits began with "sincerity," which is that hidden, private factor with which we have to live.
Next those laymen listed "humility." The third
item of character was "integrity, honesty." Examples of honesty, as stated by those surveyed, included money, personal purity, business dealings,
reports of church attendance, illustrations stated as

if personal incidents, and in performance of duties such as study and visitation. Why has the expression "ministerially speaking" developed? Only personal hungers to be authentic and to serve Jesus supremely can discipline and motivate us in this regard.

We would soon recognize that such truthfulness arises from a vital, personal relationship with the true God. Malachi stated it this way, "He walked with me in peace and equity" (v. 6c). The private communion springs from within, from authentic desires. The sweetness of fellowship with God encourages meditation of His instructions and expressions of our hearts. Jesus prayed regularly, not in spurts. He faced crises successfully because He visited with the Father regularly before tragedy struck. Many leaders need the refreshing thrust of commitment to daily devotion, not for sermons but for self.

Responsibility of Influence

To hear the prophet's word causes us to examine ourselves when he declared, ". . . and did turn many away from iniquity" (v. 6d). Great benefit results in the lives of those who dodge the destructiveness of evil. Consequently, that degree of accomplishment satisfies us when we lead someone away from wrong. However, according to Malachi, some leaders create tremendous damage by the

reverse: "But ye are departed out of the way; ye
have caused many to stumble at the law; ye have
corrupted the covenant of Levi, saith the Lord of
hosts" (v. 8). Oh, the power of influence! Oh, the
need for attention to self that others may see our
good works and, therefore, glorify our Father in
heaven.

Often leaders long for repose from the center of
observation relative to their spiritual values and
conduct. Some propose that a double standard is
unfair, that all saints are equal in privilege and
responsibility. Leaders, however, take to themselves extra equipment: divine call for service,
training, study, and experience. These intertwine
with abilities and dedication to produce leadership. In the Hebrew law, official positions carried
corresponding responsibility, the sins of rulers call-
ing for more expensive offerings (Lev. 4:3,27,32).
James wrote, "My brethren, be not many masters,
knowing that we shall receive the greater condemnation" (3:1). Applying Paul's argument to the individual confronts the seriousness of privilege.
"Thou therefore which teachest another, teachest
thou not thyself?" (Rom. 2:17-24). Paul specified
examples such as preaching not to steal or not to
commit adultery but practicing them. Then the
tragic consequences must be written, "For the
name of God is blasphemed among the Gentiles
through you, as it is written" (v. 24).

Dare we try to live today privately with convictions the apostle Paul exhibited? Can our free-wheeling society, with its excusing methods, be impressed with sincere consecration which concerns itself with influence? Paul stated, "But when ye sin so against the brethren, and wound their weak conscience, ye sin against Christ. Wherefore, if meat make my brother to offend, I will eat no flesh while the world standeth, lest I make my brother to offend" (1 Cor. 8:12-13).

Dr. Swor's conclusion bears repeating for our enriching uplift.

The scope of the minister's responsibility is vast; the load he is called upon to bear is tremendous; the demands of the people are unending; the challenge of his task is ceaseless. With no more than the motivations which impel average workers in their tasks, ministers can never perform the ministry nor find the joy which God intended for their work. The minister *must have* a motivation which transcends the selfish and material; he must have a motivation which goes far beyond even the call of duty. Is there one dynamic or drive above all others which will help the minister to be in every way more nearly what God and men want him to be?[1]

Response

Because of the callousness of some leaders, God has to act in punishment. How sad for the Almighty to be forced to declare, "I have no pleasure in you, . . . neither will I accept an offering at your hand" (Mal. 1:10c). How much better to expect the commendation of our Savior, "Well done, thou good and faithful servant: thou hast been faithful over a few things, I will make thee ruler over many things: enter thou into the joy of thy lord" (Matt. 25:21). Consider the necessity of His curse stated in Malachi 2:2-3. In addition to the economic threat of crop failure, God spoke of humiliation and disgrace, ". . . and spread dung upon your faces." Walter Kaiser put it appropriately, "The poetic justice in this fair turnabout of events which were done with such hypocrisy can be captured by our idiom that the priests would be left with egg on their faces! Everyone would begin to demean and to belittle them and the priesthood in general. The ministry would be held up to contempt, scorn, and mocking jokes because people would place little stock in such transparently false worship."[2] See Malachi 2:9 for an additional insight.

Leaders must maintain emotional balance and operate from a base of honestness and sincerity with themselves. They can do this and live with a wholesome tension of hungering to honor God above self. Samson's tragedy need not creep up on any of us, "And he wist not that the Lord was departed from him" (Judg. 16:20). Paul kept the guard on himself and declared: "I therefore so run, not as uncertainly; so fight I, not as one that beateth the air: But I keep under my body, and bring it into subjection: lest that by any means, when I have preached to others, I myself should be a castaway" (1 Cor. 9:26-27).

A new look at leadership thrusts us into the joy of effective service. The marvelous fellowship with the Master strengthens us for the winding path. Bishop Ralph S. Cushman expressed the drive of many hearts as follows:

> I do not ask
> That crowds may throng the temple,
> That standing room be priced;
> I only ask that as I voice the message
> They may see Christ!
>
> I do not ask
> For churchly pomp or pageant,
> Or music such as wealth alone can buy;
> I only ask that as I voice the message
> He may be nigh!
>
> I do not ask
> That men may sound my praises
> Or headlines spread my name abroad;
> I only pray that as I voice the message
> Hearts may find God!
>
> I do not ask
> For earthly place or laurel,
> Or of this world's distinctions any part;
> I only ask, when I have voiced the message,
> My Saviour's heart![3]

Notes

1. Chester E. Swor, "The Minister from the Layman's Viewpoint," Tharp Lectures, New Orleans Baptist Theological Seminary, 20-22 Feb. 1951.

2. Walter C. Kaiser, Jr., *Malachi God's Unchanging Love* (Grand Rapids, Mich.: Baker Book House, 1984), pp. 57-58.

3. Ralph Spauling Cushman, "The Parson's Prayer," *Masterpieces of Religious Verse*, ed. James Dalton Morrison (New York: Harper & Brothers Publishers, 1948), p. 499.

4
A New Look
at Worship
Malachi 1:7-14

An assembly of Christians needs a "getting started" activity. Many leaders have adopted a "Call to Worship" plan. Those incentives have been varied and should be creative to provide the best participation. Calls to worship include choral music, instrumental presentation, chimes, Scripture reading by various methods, prayers, hymn singing, and oral invitation to direct attention to the purpose for the meeting.

The elements of a worship service differ with the leaders and the congregation involved. Some insist that quiet, meditative music induces worship while others prefer a fast moving gospel hymn. Some expect a didactic style of sermonic delivery emphasizing content while others desire an excited exhortation emphasizing decision of the will. Leaders often give deliberate planning to involve the laity in active participation by meditative sections of time, responsive readings, leader-congregation alternate sections, congregational singing, and offertory presentations.

When someone writes about "The Most Wasted Hour of the Week" being the worship hour, we shudder. However, we really could afford to examine what happens in that allotted hour. Consideration includes the human element of planning, the genuine recognition of the divine Presence, and the interaction of humanity with Him.

Worship reaches beyond the public service to family and private worship. Certain qualities remain in all expressions of the sacred encounter, of course.

Attitude About Divine Worth—1:7c,13a

The accusing question confronted Malachi as the people asked, "Wherein have we polluted thee?" Self-deception seemed to be quite genuine. Because they engaged in religious activities, they assumed that it was worship. He would say what we know: that actions really do speak louder than words, even of religious content. Let us examine for personal profit any comparisons of the passage to our contemporary practices.

Students would enjoy looking at dictionary descriptions of *worship.* The root meanings arise from "worth" and "ship" which describe some object of value. Terms attendant to worship are "honor, respect, admiration." Those facets of it build on something of worth or evaluation.

While it may be true that more is caught than taught in public worship services, perhaps instruction in the worth of the Deity could pour significance into the expressive elements of prayer, singing, offering, Scripture reading, and meditation. What does God mean to you? What does the Word of God signify in your living? What does the privilege of prayer indicate to you? What does the offering time say to you? What expectation resides in one's mind concerning this encounter?

Observe that even in the question of Malachi 1:8 the person of God was the focal point rather than the bread or the altar. For they asked, "Wherein have we polluted thee?" Evaluation of divine worth accumulated from their previous estimates. Doubt about God's love served as a basic cancerous detriment because the leaders' rejection of His character (name) built upon doubt. "Like pastor, like people" has its element of truth. Consequently, the real problem in worship was the mind-set of the people.

One may collect examples from various sources to examine the genuineness or falseness of worship. The account about Cain and Abel is instructive. Abel was serious in preparation as he selected the best of his offering possibilities. Hebrews 11:4 credited Abel with a basic faith which exposed that

he was righteous inwardly. The Hebrew grammar
of Genesis 4:3 indicates that Cain merely took
some of his produce, indicating a carelessness of
selection. Cain's attempt at worship revealed a hol-
lowness of activity compared to a form without
substance.

The detailed punctuality of religious activities
by the Pharisees of Jesus' day served very little to
express true devotion. They quoted the Scripture,
said the prayers, and gave the tithe—emptily. The
Pharisee could profess his greatness as measured
by his fasting regularly and his superior external
conduct, being "thankful" that he was better than
the publican. But the justified person was the admitted sinner, humble in simple prayer with a sincere heart (Luke 18:10-14).

What do you think about God? The degree of
obedience waits for that evaluation. The degree of
enthusiasm for service grows from that evaluation.
How dependable is His nature and character relative to all of life's entanglements? The degree of
risk in faith-trust rests upon that estimate. How
serious are God's commands? The degree of commitment to engage in His appointed work springs
from that consideration. Our definition of "attitude" in this study includes conscious weighing of
evidence which surpasses a mere mental thought.

A corollary conclusion of their evaluation of God
resulted in their drudgery in worship activities

(Mal. 1:13a). What a painful exercise in futility if no good is achieved! How much religious gathering occurs with the thrill of the Divine Presence? "How tedious and tasteless the hours,/When Jesus no longer I see!" How much fussing and "oughtness" in guilt-intending exhortation do we have to bolster attendance? How many people do attend services out of duty primarily and endure it as a weariness?

The first couple hid, clothed with guilt and fear. The disciples hovered in that room for fear of the Jews and, probably, because they were confused about the Savior's death. But the refreshing presence of God electrified the surprise encounter. "Then were the disciples glad, when they saw the Lord" (John 20:20b). John Newton changed the "tedious and tasteless" to "His name yields the richest perfume,/And sweeter than music His voice;/His presence disperses my gloom/And makes all within me rejoice."

How do our actions express our convictions? Malachi declared that they reflect what we think.

Expression with Leftovers—1:8,12,13

The offerings listed constituted a total of worthless gifts. They matched the people's relation to Yahweh as determined by their opinion of His worth. The gifts could not be used by the people either to eat or to sell. They would not lose by

giving it away to God. Although some of our service may not be sick or crippled, it represents leftovers of that which we won't lose. It really doesn't
represent much expensive time. We recall that
challenging statement of David to Araunah. He
insisted on buying the threshingfloor and oxen because he determined, "Neither will I offer burnt
offerings unto the Lord my God of that which cost
me nothing" (2 Sam. 24:24*b*).

Motives for giving determine values. Jesus
warned that gifts which in themselves were valu-
able could be deceitfully used. For He said that if
they are given for drawing attention to oneself,
that is all the reward to be expected (Matt. 6:1-2).
Ananias and Sapphira gave some money, pretending to be completely dedicated to God in it. But
Peter declared that they had lied to God (Acts 5:4).
Paul gave the right order for righteous giving
when he wrote: "first gave their own selves to the
Lord" (2 Cor. 8:5). Didn't our wonderful Savior
clarify authentic worship when He pointed out the
poor widow with her small gift? Others gave of
their abundance, what they could do without; she
gave her whole living (Luke 21:1-4).

I drew deep satisfaction from extending myself,
even uncomfortably. A friend needed me to spend
a few hours with his father who was in the hospital
in another city. My schedule was already crammed
full. The next two days would find my family mak-

ing a trip by car over several hundred miles, consuming hours and energy before a strenuous weekend of church services. But I really wanted to do it; I could not let my friend even suspect that I was pressured because he would have asked someone else. He needed me. I really wanted to share myself—not my money to hire a nurse, but me. My friend trusted his much-loved father to my attention and care. I needed that. Can I learn that my love for God is like that—self-giving?

How can the value of the gifts be estimated? Offer them to some human from whom you desire a favorable response (Mal. 1:8). The offerings, as representing the worshiper, became contemptible as something rotten or "corrupt." Thus it pictured a sacred altar furnished with "polluted" materials which was an affront to the God of love and holiness.

Contents of Emptiness—1:10

"God has a pastor for us out there somewhere" is a normal statement regularly expressed by church people. The assumption is that God is obligated to furnish every church a choice servant. The people seldom consider that their degree of responsiveness or their treatment of a staff worker would determine God's assignments.

We must be very cautious in pretending to know the future relative to a church or to God's manner of treating a situation. Malachi, however, quoted Yahweh as desiring the Temple closed and the altar empty. Such a horrible thought would shock the average Jew, likewise, the average churchman.

To grasp the magnitude of this proposal, one remembers the reason for the Temple (2 Sam. 7:1 *ff*.). Solomon's magnificent prayer in the dedication service is a theological masterpiece (1 Kings 8). Many spiritual experiences occurred in the Temple (Isa. 6:1-8). The Temple constituted a unifying influence and a reminder of Yahweh.

To close the doors of the Temple would indicate the cessation of worship and the withdrawal of Yahweh's presence and blessings (1 Kings 8:27-30). "Icabod," meaning "the Glory has departed," remains a most serious situation (1 Sam. 4:21-22). Humanity cannot accurately determine specific applications, but we ought to recall the possibility of the removal of the church ("lampstand," Rev. 2:5, RSV).

People reacted with similar horror when Jesus attacked misuse of the Temple by hypocritical, empty worship. He charged, "It is written, My house shall be called the house of prayer; but ye have made it a den of thieves" (Matt. 21:13; see also John 2:13-17).

The first use of "for nought" (italics in KJV) is not in the Hebrew text. The second use of it (with altar) translates a word meaning "in vain, empty." It thus speaks of empty forms of worthless acts of worship.

What could produce such an awful divine indictment? The offensive acts of ritual reflected cynicism toward Yahweh ("despise my name") by defective (deplorable) sacrifices. The guidelines for the sacrificial system indicated that offerings intended to show fellowship, penitence, and the covenant commitment (Lev. 1:4; 5:5; 16:21-22). Samuel had previously stated the priority: "Hath the Lord as great delight in burnt offerings and sacrifices, as in obeying the voice of the Lord? Behold, to obey is better than sacrifice, and to hearken than the fat of rams" (1 Sam. 15:22). But empty forms of religious activities only pretend to be worship. Really, it is blasphemy.

Expectation of Divine Favor—1:9-10,14

Would their governor accept their sick sacrifices? Interpretations differ whether this is a degree of irony or a genuine call to seek God. From the context of the normal, expected refusal of verse 8 and the divine desire to shut the Temple of verse 10, the request of verse 9 is probably sarcasm. True repentance and call for mercy would gain a divine response always. But no such interest appears in any of the context. The question expects a negative answer.

As strange as it may seem, it remains true that

people expect God to accept them any time and in any condition. Common definition of *love* implies divine favor without regard to righteous requirements.

God's rejection of worthless worship appeared in verses 10 and 13. Isaiah also had expressed the same (1:10-15). Amos preached similar strong condemnation for useless religious acts (5:21-24). "Great fear came upon all them that heard these things" when the couple worshiped hypocritically (Acts 5:5). Jesus even referred to correction at the altar in human relations to be acceptable (Matt. 5:23-24).

Many people discover surprises relative to God's holy requirements for acceptability. He is not to be taken for granted, to be presumed upon. He can punish as well as forgive.

Reception of Yahweh—1:11,14*b*

Three major interpretations arise concerning Yahweh and worship in heathen lands. Some think that the reference is to sincere worship by devout Jews scattered throughout the world. Malachi's purpose would thus be to challenge his people, who lived under more suitable conditions, to match their relatives' serious devotion.

Others believe that the reference projects that Yahweh accepts the sincerity of the untrained heathen, although they worship their own false gods.

A New Look at Worship   69

Malachi's charge would thus emphasize the contrast of the heathen's sincerity and the Jews' hypocrisy.

A different view seems more consistent with the
whole biblical revelation. Elements within the
non-Jewish world could have converted to Yah-
wism. The reference need not require total submission (or even large numbers) of heathen to be
applicable. Biblical history had listed individuals
who had turned to Yahweh while residing outside
Israelite territory. Such people include Mel-
chizedek (Gen. 14:18-22), Jethro (Ex. 18:1-12),
Rahab (Josh. 2:1-11), Ruth (Ruth 1:16), and the
Ninevites (Jonah 3:5).

The divine purpose of universal witness had
been explicitly stated to Abram to include all families of the earth. Other prophets had proclaimed
that Yahweh was the God of all the earth. Malachi
had spoken about the missionary impetus in verse
5. His people should not have been surprised at the
inclusion of Gentiles in His concerns.

No group should expect to have a monopoly on
God's favor. He is eager to include everyone, but
He is not bound to limit Himself to anyone. Those
who ignore His will in obedient worship cannot
remain His instrument of service. May all present-
day believers take notice with reverent response.

5
A New Look
at Marriage/Divorce
Malachi 2:10-16

A certain eleven-year-old girl broke out into a rash as soon as she got near a boy. Most girls tingle all over. But her parents tried to shelter her in a girl's school. She said, "Boys are nasty and horrid." Maybe she could learn differently and remove her rash. Maybe others have similar problems that are unseen which affect marriage.

After we have considered relative factors, I shall ask that you count how many happy homes and how many unhappy homes you can in two minutes. A happy home does not have to be stress free or problem free. Pleasantness will not control the emotions constantly. Mates ought not be expected to be in agreement always. Irritants in others' habits and personalities remain in this life. Children will not make the choices that their parents would, or the grades in school, or the priorities of what should be important.

What elements must abide in order to classify

one as a happy home? Do family members want to be with each other? Do family members desire to support each other? Are interests respected? Are concerns of one member also a concern of another member? Is room available for aloneness and individual interests without threatening reactions?

Would you prefer to label such homes "successful" rather than "happy"? Either way, count the contrasting ones that come to mind in the next two minutes.

Everyone will admit that homemaking (home building) crowds our needs for today. With so many group activities prevalent, however, few people realize that the individual family must chart its own course. Exceedingly few influences in our society attempt to strengthen the home. Most demand time, energy, and resources away from the home. So, what shall we do?

Let us determine to spend courageously whatever it takes to build solidly a successful home. We can learn from others both what to do and what to avoid. We can face realities and expect reasonable cooperation from each other within our human frailties. We can draw upon divine wisdom and intervention.

Malachi confronted laxness in attention to homemaking. Let us examine his discussion for anticipated benefit (2:10-16).

A Lordship Matter—2:10

What interest does God have in our having happy homes? What concept of marriage and God do most people possess: rules, punishment, drudgery or guidance, resources, and exhilaration?

Malachi approached the home-life problem as a concern of Yahweh. The situation of that day will not be identical with the varied ones of our century. However, parallel truths can benefit those who search for substance and resource. Although absolute, definitive delineation of the topic is not expected here, morsels of enrichment are contained herein for those desiring to discover.

The sovereignty of God instills within us the confidence of His greatness (Mal. 1:10). Malachi used the topic to emphasize the solidarity of Jewish kinship ("brother"). Damage to one person equaled damage to the whole. Beyond the current emphasis of "each doing his own thing," much should be said of corporateness: nation, church, and family. A person has both privilege and responsibility for being a part of a whole. Thus, scriptural teachings of filial obligations clamor for attention. Notice these references: "Honour thy father and mother" (Eph. 6:2), "Obey your parents" (6:1), "Wives, submit . . . husbands, love" (5:22-25), "Provoke not your children to wrath: but bring them up in the nurture and admonition of the Lord" (6:4), and the care of widows by family members (1 Tim. 5:16).

Corresponding truths shine forth concerning relationships within the church as a body (1 Cor. 12:13-27; in 1 Cor. 3:16-17 the "ye" is plural, and in 1 Cor. 6:19 the "ye" is singular). These teach that the Holy Spirit dwells within the individual Christian and also in the church.

Marriage to partners who serve heathen gods receive strong condemnation (Mal. 2:12). The prophet's word was that one "hath married the daughter of a strange god" (v. 11). Those who desire successful homes consider the spiritual qualities of prospective mates. For religious values are exceedingly deep and determine many other elements of life.

The point of mutual interest for mates would be the sovereign Creator. All devoted individuals could agree on attachment to Him. From that common viewpoint, individuals could see how to evaluate other factors of life. Consequently, homemakers should explore the matchless resources from God's provisions and His eagerness to share. Resources include guidance for the future in the selection of mates, providential arrangement of circumstances, and miraculous intervention into personality compatability.

Lordship includes trust in divine wisdom expressed in the admonitions for conduct. Rather than seeing instructions as unduly restrictive, one would expect a goal of benefits to be intended by the Creator. Thus, marriage within such religious context proposes to be healthy, wise, and beneficial to the participants (Deut. 7:3-4).

Contemporary homemaking expresses wisdom in recognizing similar divine pronouncements. Psalm 127:1 may use the term *house* to refer to any project, but it surely can apply to family concerns: "Except the Lord build the house, they labour in vain that build it." Likewise, the importance of a couple being motivated by deep, common values exposes the significance of mutual religious convictions. Note that the relation of Christ and Satan must demonstrate mutual contrasts. So, Paul declared such in 2 Corinthians 6:15-16. Because religion may well be humanity's greatest driving force, it should be considered essential in anticipating a harmonious marriage.

Lordship goes beyond drawing upon divine resources for successful homemaking. It expands to submission to divine instruction. Thus, Christian couples exhibit alertness to search God's Word for marital guidelines. A few such admonitions are Matthew 19:1-12; Ephesians 5:21-33; and Colossians 3:18-25. General character qualities also stabilize one for successful relationships (Col. 3:5-17; Eph. 4:17-32; Rom. 12:1-2,9-13).

What help remains for homes with strained relations? Billy Graham advised the sincere dependence upon God in actively rebuilding marital interests. No simple answer displays itself. God may employ various instruments for self-evaluation. He may also use different counselors for prescribed alterations for individual and family improvements. But, nevertheless, God stays interested and effective in human dealings.

A man wrote to Graham with this story. "We are separated. And I am afraid we have hurt each other out of anger, saying untrue things about each other. We both would like to get back together, but it will be so hard for us to trust each other. I don't know if it is worth the effort."

Graham replied that God wanted the marriage to succeed. Although it would not be easy, he recommended that they rebuild on the only solid foundation—God. Each needed the Savior personally. From divine forgiveness, each should request divine help in overcoming pride and distrust. Graham suggested other practical human actions: acknowledging wrong against the mate, expressions of love, sensitivity to other's needs, and guarding against anger and careless statements.[1]

Many people expect God to control miraculously any family frictions. Others ignore the divine concern and power in building marital success. To turn it all over to the Lord is to misunderstand the faith-work principle. To omit God is to exhibit practical atheism. Malachi indicated that the people's disregard for God, as previously stated, spilled into their homes. The mistreatment of mates resulted from lack of seriousness about God's will and instructions for the home. Let us learn and heed!

Because an ounce of prevention is worth more than a pound of cure, let us emphasize to the never-married that God is worth including in their lives. Can the individual trust God to help mate selection? Can the devout Christian rest in assurance that God can work circumstances for the discovery of a mate? A person need not propose that only one mate in all the world meets divine approval. But one certainly can depend on God, who knows what is in each person, to lead by inward impression and by methods of evaluation to a suitable companion.

Estimating the value of a good home will produce willingness to exert effort both in planning and securing it. "This Is a Shelter" was the caption of an advertisement in a newspaper. Below those words was a picture of a simple house and these sentences: "This is not a fallout shelter. It is a human shelter. It protects people from the sun, rain, wind, and cold. Put love into it, and it becomes a home." A Tennessee mountain lad won a contest sponsored by a national organization for the best definition of a better home. He wrote, "A better home is a place my dad is proud to support, my mother loves to take care of, and we like to be in. It is a place to grow old in."

A family is described by the following article whose author is unknown:

A family is a PLACE to cry and laugh and vent frustrations, to ask for help and tease and yell, to be touched and hugged and smiled at.

A family is PEOPLE who care when you are sad, who love you no matter what, who share your triumphs, who don't expect you to be perfect, just growing with honesty in your own direction.

A family is a CIRCLE where we learn to like ourselves, where we learn to make good decisions, where we learn to think before we do, where we learn integrity and table manners and respect for other people, where we are special, where we share ideas, where we listen and are listened to, where we learn the rules of life to prepare ourselves for the world.

The world is a PLACE where anything can happen. If we grow up in a loving family we are ready for the world.

The urgency of maximum effort by everyone concerned, family members, churches, schools, exhibits itself by recognizing the pressures against successful homemaking. A survey of magazine articles' titles demonstrates stressful factors upon the family: "Nine Reasons for Marriage," "End of a Marriage," "Marriage Is not for Children," "The War on the American Family," "Child Rearing: It Is Getting Harder," and "Problems Confront Families."

Christians have bases for hope. God will guide sincere couples in courtship and planning marriage. He will support honest efforts of unselfishness in developing frameworks for secure families. His intervention into personalities and circumstances to strengthen relationships reflect eagerness to lift human desires. His teachings, when seriously received into conduct, grow individuals with whom successful living may be achieved. A sad article about postponed activities was entitled, "There Wasn't Time." Mother was going to read the story, letting him turn the pages as if reading it himself, but she had to wax the bathroom, and there wasn't time. Daddy was going to watch him play ball, but the car had to be tuned, and there wasn't time. The family was to pose for a Christmas picture, but sister couldn't wait, and there never was time. Families benefit from scheduling time for each other. Neglect is poison.

Mistreatment of Mate—2:14b,16

Divorce can kidnap good people. Separation may be the only (or the best) alternative. Staying together only because of a command in the Bible can be useless since unity internally would be broken. The togetherness would thus be artificial because of the reality of division in interests

preventing their becoming "one." However, staying together in sincere obedience to God (as one
understands it), trusting divine activity in resolv-
ing conflicts, and looking for divine guidance and
strength can be beneficial.

The necessity of divorce causes tears and scars.
Divorced people usually wish that it had not been
necessary. Those same people usually regret the
experience. They recommend that others do everything possible to prevent the situations that
cause divorce. Consequently, they urge careful examination and planning before entering marriage
although so many divorced persons repeat the process.

Textual material in Malachi spoke to the immediate problem, not to the complicated involvements of our times. The charge lodged against the
man for mistreatment of "the wife of thy youth,
against whom thou has dealt treacherously: yet is
she thy companion, and the wife of thy covenant"
(2:14). Women found themselves in hopeless soci-
etal and economic predicaments in those days.
God therefore laid serious responsibility upon the
man to care for his mate. In our day mutual obligations of equal seriousness challenge the home
which desires divine support. Each mate faces vital
contribution to benefit the other mate and, consequently, to the success of the partnership.

What effect does relations between mates have

upon an individual's fellowship with God? Obviously, many people never consider any connection, dividing the sacred and the secular. But the tenor of the whole revelation of God presents a tremendously enlightening picture. For Malachi declared that mistreatment was a "profaning [of] the covenant" (v. 10). Attendant factors involved actions which "profaned the holiness of the Lord" (v. 11). Rather shocking and alarming came the statements that Yahweh would cut off the person that so mistreated another and who then tried to offer an offering (v. 12). The prophet continued his description of a form of worship (empty) which included great emotion and the center item of sacrifice: the altar. Boldly stood the result: divine rejection (v. 13). Why? "Wherefore?" Because of awful actions to mates! What's the relation? Have our couples ever discovered this? Would this greatly revise the concept of spirituality by present-day religious people?

The same truth can be stated two ways. One acknowledges that an individual's disposition toward persons reveals one's concept of God. When one serves another with either expression—love or hate, respect or disrespect, honor or dishonor— one exhibits the degree to which one cares about divine instruction. For as God's plan for people becomes our map of operations, He can lead and support our attitudes, or otherwise.

Correspondingly, our evaluation of God will be reflected in our dealings with other people. Openness and freedom with God permits Him to identify with us inwardly in the decision-making facilities of personality. Later revelation exposes that sin against a brother is sin against Christ which is disturbingly serious (1 Cor. 8:12). Parallel attitudes toward other persons and God remain reasonable in 1 John 4:7-21. Romans 14—15 speak similar truths of mutual respect and assistance. The strong should be thoughtful to protect the weak; the weak should be careful to accept what God has accepted in the activities of the strong.

In marriage/divorce in any age, divine concepts and wisdom operate. Individual examination and alteration spring into God's expectation of a person. Twice in our passage came the message, "Take heed to your spirit" and act correctly (Mal. 2:15-16). Change, improvement, and self-control grant us the options to determine our future. We possess no automatic exemptions due to being helpless victims of circumstances. A mate sometimes discovers an impossible situation because the companion rejects all expressions of care, love, and compatibility. But every effort should be made before surrendering to failure.

Conscientious Commitment—2:14-16

Christians today rejoice with the emphasis given our singles, both divorced and never married. We convey the love and respect that they deserve. We sympathize with them in the damage incurred. We stand by them in their reconstruction. We listen to them in the interest of healing. We learn from them in order to assist others, perhaps to avoid similar predicaments.

A major element required for today's living is an old-fashioned idea of commitment. Admittedly, youth grow up in a throw-away world, enjoying the luxury of convenient disposables. Construction contractors burn or haul good lumber to trash dumps, for it is cheaper to destroy it than to pay workers to save it and to buy space for storage. Think of the disposable items you encounter: eating utensils, graduation robes, medical supplies, and others. People used to change dollars on shirts, as well as darn socks, to gain longer wear. Time costs too much to do that now. A mental transfer occurs to be likewise as casual and flippant with employment, debts, and friendships. If it isn't convenient, discard it because people will agree or, at least, understand.

Malachi's message fits well today's need: "Take heed to your spirit, that ye deal not treacherously." Call upon intelligent planning and deliberate deci-

sions with a determination to succeed. An inter-
viewer asked mountain climbers if they would
make it to the top. Most answered rather smugly,
"I'll try," or "I'll give it that old college effort." One
man replied with a tone of definiteness, "Yes, I
will." Although not the strongest, he achieved it.
He bolstered his desire with total determination.

The acceptance of obligations seriously, intelli-
gently, and deliberately would help prevent many
marital failures. Employment contracts involve
some distasteful elements. Quitting too easily only
removes the immediate discomfort. The payment
of debts often requires self-sacrificing of some less
important desire. Who should plan expected financial payments according to priority needs and
wants?

Concerning homemaking, similar commitments
become necessary. One's time must be shared with
another. Money must be spent for the common
good. Risks become realities for which one must be
willing to sacrifice personal desires to care for
emergencies: sickness or accidents which strain
time, finances, and emotions. Partners may have or
may develop personality defects which hurt the
other. To learn to remedy or to adjust confronts
the alternative to discard it. Deliberate commitments include consciously comparing personal interests to determine the mutuality or compatibility
of them. This speaks to humanity's deepest motiva-

tional interests—spiritual devotion and its expression. Does each prospective partner in marraige share these?

Realism dictates that "for worse" might really occur. Preparation for such resides in serious commitment. "Until death do us part" projects a lengthy future of many hills, often without the wind at our back.

Protection notices that dangers arrive in subtle forms. External pressures often drive couples together as the strong wind made the man clutch his coat. Internal neglects permit drifting apart, causing unseen cracks which grant entrance to destructive intrusions. Sadness, produced by preventable tragedy, entered the home of P. H. Danks. He was basically a self-taught musician who wrote successfully both secular and sacred presentations. He composed over thirteen hundred individual numbers. He discovered a poem in a Wisconsin farm journal for which he offered three dollars. The editor was so pleased in finding an admirer that he gave Danks an entire collection of poems. Danks turned one of those into loving, sentimental tribute to his wife. For she and he had built a home of happiness in spite of poverty. That song became one of America's most famous sentimental ballads: "Silver Threads Among the Gold." Two million copies of sheet music sold. It was revived in vaudeville with outstanding commercial success, selling a million more copies. Unfortunately, Danks had sold this song outright for a pittance and never profited from its fabulous income. Moreover, the couple separated the year after the song became popular. It is his only production that is remembered. Danks died in poverty, alone, in a dismal rooming house in Philadelphia. Near his bed was a copy of the hit song with his last recorded words written across the copy: "It's hard to die alone." A friend later wrote, "A wrong spirit toward money wrecked a home that poverty could never weaken."

Homemaking finds shelter in love and commitment that external luxuries and pressures cannot destroy. Couples must live in alertness to corrosive spots that will eat destructive pits in their romance. Viewpoints register. Optimism seeks for cooperative efforts to remove irritating habits of mates. Pessimism expects suspicious acts. A man regularly left the cap off the toothpaste. That bothered the wife something fierce, and she said so constantly. One day the solution struck his responsive chord. He very conscientiously replaced the cap every time he used the toothpaste. She did notice. After a week, she asked, "Why have you quit brushing your teeth?"

In repairing strained structures of a home, the couple must decide whether they really desire to survive together or merely want data to justify a split. A visitor commented about the beautiful oak tree in a family's yard and received the story. "We were having friction between us and thought that maybe we might as well call it quits. We had planted some young trees, so we agreed to let the little oak show us. As long as it lived, we would stay together. The neighbors caught both mates carrying water to the little oak." Repair will be long, difficult, and painful. But isn't the home worth all the efforts and any cost?

Notes

1. Billy Graham, *Shreveport Times*, 6 Nov. 1985, Sec. B, p. 2. Used by permission.

6
A New Look
at Morality
Malachi 2:17 to 3:6

This descriptive declaration made its way into the monologue of a popular comedian: "I'm sick and tired." Scholars learn that understanding such expressions goes beyond etymological exegesis. That similar reality gave rise to another antagonistic complaint by Malachi's people, "Wherein have we wearied him?" (Mal. 2:17).

Two practices had disgusted Yahweh. And how contemporary for twentieth century citizens they are! First, confusion of moral evaluations left distorted distinctions. Second, recognition of the fact that God really cared about sincere conduct so that He would punish had drifted across the horizon.

Limited Insight of God's Moral Evaluation—2:17c

Dangers between hypocritical legalism and permissive erosion of differences between good and evil plague our decision making. Many of Jesus'

problems with the Pharisees engaged His emphasizing motives (internal) in contrast to actions (external). Some good elements of life became wrong
in their misuse, for example, fasting, prayer, and
tithing. Legalists stayed within the specified limits
with actions; but they often transgressed the prin-
ciples of obedience because of insincerity. In determining our personal conduct, we want to avoid
the picky criticism of others as measured by a stiff,
artificial rule. Individuals, however, must live with
their understanding of moral matters as they privately relate to God.

The people of Malachi's audience were not seeking that devoted insight of purity. Their concept of
God had repeatedly been negative. Here they declared that God did not care about evil; they
figured that He would accept any kind of conduct.
The brazenness astonishes us. We find it in actions
today, however, for some live as if to say: "You can
read it right out of the Book, but I'll do as I desire."
Our society has moved from delineation of sin and
from serious consciousness of any divine penalty.
This partly comes from extremes of listing a few
pet, external sins while neglecting condemnation
of attitudinal, internal sins of the disposition. Thus,
church discipline fell beyond the bounds of exact
measurement for enforcement.

Our benefits from this passage will be derived
from the degree of sincere, personal hunger to

honor God by refraining from evil. A New Testament passage still challenges us when the Greek says: " 'Test things that differ,' i.e., good and bad" (*The Expositor's Greek Testament*, Phil. 1:9). For many things look good, appear acceptable, except for something different. For example, Eve saw that the fruit was good for food, just as Jesus also gave food to hungry people. But to eat food at the time and in association with Satan would not discern the "things that differ," making it evil.

What defines gambling? Some propose that farming, stock market, and marriage are all gambling because of the risks involved. Have the corners of right become rounded by rational rubbing? Does geographical mores really affect moral standards? Is right always right? Is gambling merely taking chances, or does it require desire to profit from investment? Do good goals justify gambling?

A pastors' conference in Georgia passed resolutions against the PTA having a cake walk to raise money. At another occasion, all ticket stubs at a basketball game were eligible for the drawing. Holders of selected tickets could try their skill at free throws. Those getting a certain percentage of baskets would have their ticket stubs put back into the box for a final drawing at the end of the season to get a color television. Does that procedure differ significantly from the Christian organization selling tickets to a presentation. All ticket stubs were

placed in the box for prizes. They had so much fun
and entertainment that it surely didn't seem like
gambling. Because the individual was encouraged
to buy many tickets to raise the chance of winning
prizes, the individual had to decide whether it was
gambling. But it differed from a common raffle in
that entrance for the show required one ticket.
Does the environment of fun and scholarship fund-
ing justify the practice? Does the admonition apply
which says, "Abstain from all appearance of evil"
(1 Thess. 5:22), or is that question raising radical
legalism? Is bingo for charity justified, especially if
it is considered paying for entertainment?

The state legislature of New York legalized gambling for nonprofit and religious groups. But the
district attorney of the borough of Queens in New
York City said that some churches were operating
large-scale gambling operations. The churches did
not have gambling equipment, nor did they really
know how to operate it. They began sponsoring
"Las Vegas Nites" to raise funds for community
programs. The district attorney feared infiltration
by organized crime. Is this practice right or
wrong?

If a church holds a fair or carnival and sells beer
to boost revenues, is it holy? Does the use of illegal
drugs by religious sects change the moral element?
Did the sexual participation with holy men or holy

women in a religious rite for Baal or Aphrodite relieve it of sinfulness?

Moreover, when we raise questions of "which is worse?" do we set in motion a justification for a questionable item? Are we often seeking to replace scriptural authority for conduct with conscience-salved reasonings?

But when an individual hungers for unrestricted access to the Father, in unhindered fellowship, does one prefer to be as honestly right as knowledge will permit? People must live their private Christian lives according to their convictions sincerely derived without regard for the opinions of others. Perhaps, the motive factor dominates: Is one unduly legalistic, or is one conscientiously seeking to be as error free as humanly possible? Is one's usefulness to Deity related to one's concepts of morality? Revival in China and Korea resulted from the missionaries taking a new look at morality. They searched the Scriptures for determination of what constituted sin. They searched themselves to discover every tinge of known sin in their lives. They dealt with their own sin, not pointing out the sin of another person. They treated all sin as displeasing and destructive whether of the spirit or the flesh. Whatever excesses might have arisen, the consecrated saints moved with sincere devotion. And God rewarded with astonishing spiritual awakening.

Perhaps Malachi's audience did not confront these complexities of determining the will of God in "situational ethics." Their charge against God was that He had accepted the heathen who were evil instead of prospering the "righteous" Jew. But that philosophy remains very close to the erosion of the moral standards with which we live. Isaiah thundered one of his woes "unto them that call evil good, and good evil" (5:20a). Many other problems entangle us, such as sexual license and the home/ church code of conduct.

Limited Understanding of the Scope of God's Justice—2:17d

The question of "Where is the God of judgment?" raised the issue of God's character. The relation to the previous statement about God's accepting evil people revealed that the people exhibited sarcasm. They supposed that Yahweh was unfair in not accepting them (the righteous Israelites) with evidence in material prosperity. Their criticism of Yahweh may show a kinship to deism. They posited that He cared little for justice and dared not intervene in human affairs with rewards or judgment. By remaining detached from human involvements, God would permit evil to flourish and good to remain unrewarded. Such ideology reveals doubts or denials of an active divine government operating from character qualities.

Obviously, the expressed rejection of active divine righteousness negates spiritual enrichment from devoted allegiance. Religion and morality would travel different roads in mutual isolation. Spiritual service would serve no practical function and remain empty.

The prevailing problem revealed that the people conceived God as penalizing Israel, which claimed to be righteous, and as supporting the pagan Persians. The Pharisees considered themselves to be God's favorites. The unconverted Saul thought that he was serving God by killing the Christians. Deceived people really do accept warped ideas.

Our citizens generally follow the above-mentioned outlook. Survey statistics produce little information on this subject. A national, secular magazine recorded that while most Americans say that they believe in God, three out of four admit that they never think of Him in relation to their own lives or associate Him with their behavior. Consequently, many parents have only the slightest idea of how living their religion could determine their children's outlook.[1] In another article, David Klein wrote that Western man has lost belief in God as a personal force, as the decider of destiny, or as the ultimate judge of actions. He noted that while we still believe in right and wrong in principle, we no longer accept consciously that

we offend God by doing wrong or that we expect
His wrath.[2] Thus, human beings become their own
standards, and they live by human expectations.
The Ten Commandments become ten suggestions!

Habakkuk struggled with questions concerning
divine delay of punishing wickedness. But he
never engaged the calloused rebellion of Malachi's
contemporaries. Habakkuk built upon the holy nature of God, expecting that God would punish the
wicked (1:13). Amos put extra responsibility upon
those of enlightened, favored status when he proclaimed, "You only have I known of all the families
of the earth: therefore I will punish you for all your
iniquities" (3:2).

Corrected View of the God of Justice—3:1-5

The audience of sinful Israelites had expressed in
the foregoing passage that they expected Yahweh
to be cooperative with them, to approve their actions, and to punish others. The provocative, in-
sinuative question had been stated, "Where is the
God of judgment [justice]?" So Yahweh answered
the inquiry by announcing His personal attention
to handle the matter. The accomplishment would
not be in their immediate future to deal with those
specific individuals. But it gave opportunity for
God to speak to the broad purpose of His kingdom.
His presence would be surprising to their general

concept of approval of their heartless religion; it would be the judgment of sin, even Israel's sin.

The dark mist of human complaint against Yahweh became emblazoned with a prediction of messianic intervention. The biblical passage contains expository treasures. It offers an exegetical adventure. The careful student will enjoy pondering these verses to determine identifications of the following persons: "my messenger," "me," "the Lord," and "the messenger of the covenant." In addition, the realization in history needs to be defined. Admittedly, investigators should consult all kinds of interpreters for insight into the passage. We build on grammatical exegesis to present the spiritually devotional exposition.

In Malachi 3:1 the personal pronouns "I" and "me" designate Yahweh, the Father. "Behold" captures attention to stimulate response for an urgently important announcement.

"My messenger" translates the Hebrew word *Malachi*. The *i* is a pronominal suffix as on the words *"Eli, Eli"* of the last words of Jesus meaning "my" with "El" (God). The term *Malach* refers to angel or messenger. Because of its occurrence here, some interpreters have chosen to deny the word to be a personal name of the prophet in Malachi 1:1. Jesus specifically quoted this reference in identifying it with John the Baptist (Matt. 11:7-15). The prophetic forerunner of this statement had been Isaiah 40:3-5. All four Gospel writers affirmed it (Matt. 3:1-3; Mark 1:3; Luke 3:4; and John 1:23). The identification with Elijah from the later Malachi 4:5 passage came in the angelic message to Zacharias, the father of John the Baptist (Luke 1: 17,76). Jesus reiterated it (Matt. 11:14; 17:10-14).

The function of the messenger to prepare the way related to the Oriental practice for the arrival of kings. As we have secret service preparation to protect parade routes, so they had the roads cleared of brush, rocks, holes, and other obstructions. It enabled the townspeople to ready themselves. For John the Baptist and the Messiah, it meant moral and spiritual inventory involving heart preparation to receive His instruction. Therefore, the Baptist's declaration resounded, "Repent ye."

Observe the identification of the person referred to as "the Lord," "his temple," "the messenger of the covenant," and "he" in the clause "he shall come." Because of the direct quotation from "the Lord of hosts," this person is distinct from Yahweh. The term *adon* ("lord") means "sir," "lord," "master" and could describe anyone of superior status, as Sarah called Abram "lord." Thus, it does not spell the personal name "Yahweh." But it designates Deity with the use of the definite article (Ex. 23:27; 34:32; Isa. 1:24). Moreover, Messiah was so defined in Psalm 110:1: "Yahweh said to my lord." His temple must refer to the spiritual relationship (the image of God, the heart) as one phase of "kingdom" also does. The messenger of the covenant was the special theophanic manifestation of Yahweh who was active throughout Old Testament history (Gen. 16:7; 28:10-17; 32:24-30; Ex. 3:1-14; 23:20; 33:11; and numerous others). Micah 5:2 declares that the "ruler" to come to Bethlehem was the One who had been active from old times, even from everlasting.[3]

With a divine Person being distinct from the Father (Yahweh), we have an easy-flowing recognition of functional oneness void of conflict or competition. Marriage is pictured as two persons becoming one in purpose, intent, and desires while remaining separate persons (Matt. 19:1-6). Jesus could say "I and my Father are one" (John 10:30), although each was separate at Jesus' baptism (Matt. 3:13-17). Similarly, Jesus and the Spirit relate (Col. 1:27 compared with Col. 3:1). The speaker of Malachi 3:1 was Yahweh, the Lord of hosts, to whom the pronoun "me" referred. But, obviously, the messenger preparing the way for "me" was preparing the way for Messiah, distinct from Yahweh in person. Understanding of this truth could help the Jews grasp reality of oneness in their *Shema*, "Hear, O Israel: The Lord our God is one Lord" (Deut. 6:4).

"But who may abide the day of his coming?"

(Mal. 3:2a). His coming would signal judgment, but it would not be the judgment on others as the scoffers expected (2:17). Allusions to fire and soap picture judgment and cleansing. The prophetic ministry had regularly declared the "day of the Lord" which had four elements: (1) judgment, (2) all nations, (3) salvation of believers, and (4) the kingdom of God. Study Obadiah 15-21; Joel 1:15; 2:28-31; 3:16-17; Amos 5:18; 9:15 (combined with Acts 15:16-18). Also, see "in that day" throughout the prophets. The Joel passage was quoted by Peter at Pentecost as beginning its fulfillment with Jesus (Acts 2:16-22).

The figures of refining fire and launderer's soap indicate that beyond the testing will come a true, clean product—a remnant of believers. Whether Rahab, Ruth, or individuals through all ages, this principle of judgment on sin and salvation of believers has demonstrated God's moral operation of His nature. The participants of Malachi's age or ours would confront the same divine activity. Consequently, the message about a future Messiah found application to Malachi's hearers. Indeed, He spoke to achieve a response of trust: "That they may offer unto the Lord an offering in righteousness" (Mal. 3:3). He predicted the achievement of acceptable service to the holy God (v. 4). We can reasonably assume that those facts would apply to them and to us as would the punishment upon listed sins of verse 5.

Corrected View of God's Faithfulness—3:6

Struggle with sin and its remedy has been difficult to grasp. Moses tried several corrective measures after the awful rebellion relative to the golden calf (Ex. 32). The covenant and the Ten Commandments had not given answers to broken commandments and "high-handed" sins of the heart. In addition to the revelation of individual responsibility (Ex. 32:33), Yahweh proceeded to state clearly the only medium for dealing adequately with sin: His moral qualities (Ex. 34:6-7). His nature remains because it is not a fact learned or an attitude to be remembered; it is God—constantly and permanently.

The dependable character of Yahweh has been taught and assumed by us. Think about how brightly illuminating and securely refreshing that truth speaks to those whose gods are fickle and changeable. To attempt to play a game while referees change the rules would be frustrating, likewise with life. For God to declare that He does not change is to exhibit that He does not need to change in order to improve. He is dependable. He is the same yesterday, today, and forever (Heb. 13:8).

References to God's repenting (changing) describe His turning from a proposed course of action. He need not engage repentance as in our human terminology of turning from sin. Each context of the statements expressing divine repentance speaks of His changing judgment intent or method of judgment (Gen. 6:6; 1 Sam. 15:29; Jonah 3:1-10).

God's wonderful character constituted hope for the accusing audience of Malachi's community. Israel's unfaithfulness had produced the necessary punishment, recently realized in their Bayblonian captivity. But God's lovingkindness continued His activity to reach them as demonstrated by the sending of Malachi. May we all rejoice in renewed assurance of our God's stability!

Notes

1. Ardis Whitman, "What Not to Tell a Child About God," *The Reader's Digest*, Feb. 1962, pp. 81-82.

2. David Raphael Klein, "*Is* There a Substitute for God?" *The Reader's Digest*, Mar. 1970, pp. 51-52.

3. For additional study of an enriching topic, see many commentaries on passages treating "The Angel of Jehovah [the Lord]." Systematized data can be found in Franklin Atkinson, *God's Goodness* (Nashville: Broadman Press, 1980), pp. 90-99; Landrum P. Leavell, *Angels, Angels, Angels* (Nashville: Broadman Press, 1973), pp. 79-87. In Malachi, see Thomas J. Delaughter, *Malachi: Messenger of Divine Love*, pp. 109-110, and Walter C. Kaiser, Jr., *Malachi: God's Unchanging Love*, p. 83.

7
A New Look
at Repentance
Malachi 3:7

Interesting games can be developed with magnets. When placed in one position, magnets repel. Small magnets were located inside little ceramic dogs. When someone tried to bring the dogs together nose to nose, they each backed away. After a magnet was reversed in one dog, they were attracted to each other, kissing nose to nose. God desires close, comfortable fellowship with mankind; mankind needs and in some ways hungers for a god (the "God-shaped vacuum"). But the natural man wars against God (Rom. 8:7) because of human selfishness, independence, and revolt-mindedness. How can alteration bring them together?

Human reasoning prefers to locate any obstruction outside self. We do that by transferring fault, such as: "The woman whom thou gavest to be with me, she gave me of the tree, and I did eat" (Gen. 3:12). Or even "The devil made me do it." Usually, circumstances, pictured as uncontrollable, get a big share of blame. A little boy was being jacked up for having gone swimming. "But," he protested, "I was tempted beyond what I could bear." "Why did you have your bathing suit on?" "Well," he replied, "I kinda thought I might be tempted above what I could stand." Cain even blamed God that his punishment was too great to bear (or that his sin was too big for God to forgive). Some thus protest that they would serve God except that His standards are too high. They feel the Christian life is too hard to live. But what is the net profit of dodging the issue—man remains away from God whom he desperately needs.

Identifying the Real Problem—3:7c

Another accusing, self-justifying question appears. "Wherein shall we return?" asked Malachi's obstinate audience. *If man and God are very far apart, surely God should do the moving,* they reasoned.

The concept of correction by means of turning or returning is the normal prophetic expression. The New Testament equivalent is "repentance." The Hebrew word *Shuv* is translated "repent" only in three Old Testament passages (1 Kings 8:47; Ezek. 14:6; and 18:30). "Turn" and "return" regularly express *Shuv*. This element reaches to the depth of genuine change. It speaks of a conscious, voluntary decision to control self at the will level. The desire for improvement surpasses emotion to convince the real self of the importance of a needed change. Consequently, the solution includes individual responsibility and personal determination to respond adequately.

Repentance penetrates much farther than many people realize. Confession brings relief from guilt and can restore some relationships. It may, however, fall short of being repentance. For a thief caught with the goods may admit, confess, to the crime without any expectation of avoiding it in the future (like a child in the cookie jar). Sorrow, remorse, and regret, although tearfully proclaimed, may only apply to consequences, such as drunkenness or traffic violations. Again, promises of good intentions may be too shallow to alter the person at the desire level, such as many New Year's resolutions (for example, dieting).

But the actual turning reveals the depth decision of self-alteration. Sackcloth for the body and remorse of the emotion must not be confused with a determined abandonment of sin and a return to God. John the Baptist demanded fruit to exhibit a change. He required those with two coats to give one to a needy person, those with food to share it, those collecting money to be honest, and others to avoid violence and false accusation while being content with their wages (Luke 3:7-14). Zacchaeus returned money and added restitution funds. Repentance is in the will, expressed by actions.

Some people confess the same sin to God every night. The age-old story about a man who regularly prayed that God would wipe the spider webs from his life illustrates this. Another person broke into his prayer with, "Lord, why not just kill the spider?"

All of the above-mentioned items may well lead to repentance. The most-used word translated "repent" in the Old Testament has basic ideas of "to pant, sigh, groan" which came to mean grieve or to feel sorrowful. It is used of God's actions as well as man's and may or may not be related to personal, moral relations. However, realization of personal detriment can bring sorrow which can produce evaluation of one's situation. Confession can bring into the open one's need which can develop into a commitment expressed by a promise. Thus, repentance can evolve in conjunction with those elements, but it should not be equated with them.

Why would people refuse to draw near to God with their sarcastic "Wherein shall we return"? They, like we, apparently deceived themselves into believing that they were correct. Moreover, many emphasize the good qualities of God's love and grace to the extent that they consider it His privilege to forgive without reason of repentance and to maintain a proper relationship with us. The holy and righteous nature of God, however, re-mains as real as His love and must require righ-teousness in people, which demands an alteration in us.

Facing the Need for Repentance—3:7a

Contrast exists between God's dependableness and man's instability in commitments. Yahweh had spoken with certainty of His steadfast love in Malachi 1:2. He had declared that it displayed it-self throughout history. Yahweh had promised to provide Messiah (Mal. 3:1). He had stated His per-fection with no need for improvement changes in the verse immediately preceding this new charge. Complaints against the goodness of Yahweh, al-though arising since the Garden of Eden events, never could establish validity.

On the other hand, a brief survey of Malachi's sermons indicates a terrible list of human sins, liv-ing contradictory to the stated will of God. The ordinances of God reveal His expressed desire for our successful living. We are not granted a specific reference date of the disobedience "from the days of your fathers." No need prevails to build a long historical heritage of rebellion. For some would have transferred guilt from themselves to their ancestors (Jer. 31:29; Ezek. 18:2). But God's con-tinuing efforts to maintain covenant relations with

Israel shine throughout the prophetic ministry (Isa. 1:2-4; Hos. 10:9; Jer. 2:1-5).

Reference to God's ordinances exhibits His concern that mankind have illumination. The need for revealed religion crashes upon us. God is far too great for frail humanity to fathom. We can only know Him to the extent that He unveils Himself. Moreover, we are far too limited to comprehend Him in our natural estate. Therefore, God acted in human history in order to teach us progressively as the race could absorb the truth. He moved into man's understanding with additional revelation because of this human weakness. For Jesus declared to Simon Peter, "Flesh and blood hath not revealed it unto thee, but my Father which is in heaven" (Matt. 16:17).

He likewise provided a competent record that we could examine reports of His dealings for our benefit. Psalm 19 extols the universality of natural revelation as well as the wonderfulness of special revelation. The expressions excite the saint who concentrates on them: "converting the soul," "making wise the simple," "rejoicing the heart," "enlightening the eyes," and "enduring for ever." The stability of God's instruction plants our hopes securely in the words of Jesus, "Till heaven and earth pass, one jot or one tittle shall in no wise pass from the law, till all be fulfilled" (Matt. 5:18).

Malachi, Jesus, James, and many others emphasized that the spoken and written Word of God must be accepted in living. You "have not kept them" (Mal. 3:7). Jesus urged the doing of them as He said, "Therefore whosoever heareth these sayings of mine, and doeth them, I will liken him unto a wise man, which built his house upon a rock" (Matt. 7:24). He contrasted the person who might indeed hear but not incorporate His words as the foolish one who builds a house on shifting sand. James was likewise straightforward in placing serious consequences on failure to live the Word. For James wrote, "But be ye doers of the word, and not hearers only, deceiving your own selves" (1:22).

To stimulate us beyond the problem of Malachi's audience, let us refresh ourselves on the value of God's Word to us. This might well cause us to feed daily within it, to study and to teach it in Sunday School faithfully, and to explain it most attractively in preaching occasions. "All Scripture is given by inspiration of God, and is profitable for doctrine, for reproof, for correction, for instruction in righteousness: That the man of God may be perfect, thoroughly furnished unto all good works" (2 Tim. 3:16-17). The building of confidence, a strong faith, results from actions other than praying for it according to Romans 10:17: "So then faith cometh by hearing, and hearing by the word of God."

Repentance may seem a foreign element in our high-tech society. We have cured so many ills with

our research. Do some people expect to discover
an all-new avenue of divine approval and relationship without human change from real, moral sin?
Others will cuddle in smug complacency, assuming innocence or automatic forgiveness, and by
their actions repeat the accusation: "Wherein shall
we return?" Is human sinfulness very real to the
twentieth century citizen? God's Word, activated
by the Holy Spirit and expressed compassionately
by friends, will still prick the sensitive chords of
our people.

Assurance in Repentance—3:7b

We need God to be active in our normal, daily
involvements. We shall enjoy life in its best dimen-
sions when we cooperate with our wise and loving
Redeemer. We need never fear getting too holy by
being separated from sin. We can repent with constant improvement from sin and yet have too
much tendency toward sin left in us. Becoming
convinced that repentance belongs to us individu-
ally might benefit our spiritual lives tremendously.

The promise of God's presence matches the special imperative—"Return unto me, and I will return unto you, saith the Lord of hosts." The New
Testament says, "Draw night to God, and he will
draw nigh to you" (Jas. 4:8). Everyone can bring to
mind examples of the wonderfulness of God's participation in our lives: strength, guidance, solace,

and cooperative ministry. This was God's answer to Moses about the difficult, practically impossible, task of delivering Israel from Egypt—"Certainly I will be with you" (Ex. 3:12). The young man named Jeremiah faced a ministry of opposition from all segments of society. This assurance registered with him, "Be not afraid of their faces: for I am with thee to deliver thee, saith the Lord" (Jer. 1:8). Our Lord thrust the young church into the expanses of worldwide missions with the same promise, "I am with you alway, even unto the end of the world" (Matt. 28:20).

Sin blasts this sweet communion. "Behold, the Lord's hand is not shortened, that it cannot save; neither his ear heavy, that it cannot hear: But your iniquities have separated between you and your God, and your sins have hid his face from you, that he will not hear" (Isa. 59:1-2). The same arises from the "recipe for revival" of 2 Chronicles 7:14. May our spiritual adventure increase in delight and effectiveness as we confront the reality of repentance in our lives.

Amid the fog of man's indifference shines God's steadfastness to encourage the confused heart. Amid the shifting sands of man's waywardness remains God's dependableness to hold the weary mind. Beyond the gloomy horizon of man's perplexities comes God's promises to restore the bedraggled life. The alarm bell of conscience must

ring to tell of God's displeasure with people's indifference to His ordinances.

Ministerial students compiled a list of items that
are important for a growing spiritual life. They
named ten elements such as Bible study, church
attendance, prayer, tithing, and witnessing. Everything named involved adding or doing. No one
mentioned any "laying aside" as Peter said (1 Pet.
2:1). Very few people consider removing defects
(sins); that's repentance. May our spiritual inventory include items to be removed as well as items to
be added for enriching cooperation with our God.

8
A New Look
at Stewardship
Malachi 3:8-12

"Churches Eye Tithing Plan as Income Booster" was the column headline on June 19, 1953. The article was by George W. Cornell, Associated Press. His report stated that big church denominations had given little attention since the turn of the century to "the Old Testament injunction that a tenth of what each man earns should be set aside as 'holy unto the Lord.'" He added, "The key to the new programs is an old idea—the tithe." Cornell quoted the Rev. T. K. Thompson, National Council of Churches, as saying, "Tithing is a great new rediscovery of this generation of Christians." Malachi stressed that tithing revealed the heart of a worshiper. Tithing is God's way of raising His children rather than man's way of raising money.

The use of finances does reveal so much about the living practices of people. Wayne Dehoney wrote that "the biographer of the Duke of Wellington, Philip Guedalla, spent many days scrutinizing and analyzing the statesman's bills and cancelled checks. He said, 'find out how a man spends his money and you will find the real man.' " Dehoney also reported that Martin Luther said that every man needed two conversions, one of the heart and another of the pocketbook.[1]

Tithing and the Devout Worshiper

The newspaper article could be interpreted as employing the tithing principle primarily to raise funds. Some churches seem to want money so desperately that they are willing to receive "tainted" money. Of course, no spiritual barometer can determine which offerings from which members would be acceptable to our Lord. But caution should prevail to prevent empty tithing which amounts to religious bribery. Neither should tithing be considered a substitute for spiritual devotion and participation in active ministry. Samuel had responded to Saul's disobedience of keeping sheep from the Amalekites in the guise of making them offerings to Yahweh. Samuel declared, "Hath the Lord as great delight in burnt offerings and sacrifices, as in obeying the voice of the Lord? Behold, to obey is better than sacrifice, and to hearken than the fat of rams" (1 Sam. 15:22). Isaiah thundered, "To what purpose is the multitude of your sacrifices unto me? saith the Lord: I am full of the burnt offerings of rams, and the fat of fed beasts; and I delight not in the blood of bullocks, or of lambs, or of he goats. When ye come to appear before me, who hath required this at your hand, to tread my courts?" (Isa. 1:11-12). Isaiah continued to describe God's great disgust with artificial worship.

Likewise, Jesus blasted such religious practice by saying, "Woe unto you, scribes and Pharisees, hypocrites! for ye pay tithe of mint and anise and cummin, and have omitted the weightier matters of the law, judgment, mercy, and faith: these ought ye to have done, and not to leave the other undone" (Matt. 23:23).

The apostle Paul put the perspective correctly when he wrote that they "first gave their own selves to the Lord, and unto us by the will of God" (2 Cor. 8:5). He added, "Every man according as he purposeth in his heart, so let him give; not grudgingly, or of necessity: for God loveth a cheerful giver" (2 Cor. 9:7).

Keeping the motives right is constant self-discipline. Some people dodge tithing by saying, "Well, if you can't give it cheerfully, it's better not to give it." But those are not the only two alternatives. One can evaluate priorities, draw near to God, and change one's uncheerful heart so that one can give gladly and gratefully. A ten-year-old boy had no trouble giving the coins which made up his tithe from his small allowance. But when he received

$87 from his grandfather's sale of a calf, he struggled with giving real dollars. His parents reminded, encouraged, and tried to persuade of spiritual relationships. Finally, his mother explained that if he just wasn't going to relay the tithe, she would have to ask Grandpa not to give any more. The boy gave it; how cheerfully, no one knows; what was learned, only he and God know. The parents wanted to train the child to practice early to honor God in material prosperity. John D. Rockefeller is said to have made the following statement, "I never would have been able to tithe my first million dollars if I had not tithed my first salary, which was $1.50 a week."

A story often has been told about a man who knelt with his pastor and committed himself to God and to tithing. His first week's pay was $10, and he gave $1. His tithe grew, even reaching $500 per week. He called his pastor for help. He wanted release from his commitment because he just couldn't afford to give so much. The pastor replied, "I'm afraid you cannot get released from the promise, but there is something we can do. We can kneel again and ask God to shrink your income so that you can afford to give a dollar."

Malachi's audience was not seeking to know God's guidance about tithing and related spiritual devotion. They had offered polluted bread and crippled animals, followed a corrupt priesthood, divorced wives, married women of pagan religions, and wearied God with false charges of His unfaithfulness. In the preceding verse (3:7), Malachi had demanded repentance and received a cold, calloused, sarcastic rebuff. So the discourse on tithing was to indicate another of their many conditions which needed change for serious spirituality.

Seriousness of God's Charge—3:8-9

Robbery is criminal. The descriptive term used here appears again only in Proverbs 22:23. The meaning "to rob, to defraud, to overreach" found its graphic use in Talmudic literature as "to take forcibly." To take from a person what rightly belongs to him is terrible. To do that from the Almighty, one's Deity, is really unthinkable, even senseless. But, because He is spirit, therefore unseen, and because He is love, therefore understanding and accepting, we subconsciously reason that "Good Old God" will overlook minor mishaps. However, Malachi stated it seriously—"Robbery." Moreover, we assume that since God is self-sufficient, He really does not suffer need from our robbing Him of material matters. In addition, He is not as recognizable to the less spiritual person as the landlord, grocer, or lending agent. But is God indeed real? Does He truly command from love? Must He act to reprimand dishonesty?

Many churches in New Orleans have "poor boxes" for the worshipers to deposit funds for the specially needy. Our church folks gasped in astonishment when thieves broke into the "poor" box of neighboring churches. "How low can anyone get?" Churches have been robbed often in these days, apparently without pain of conscience. But churchgoers must face the reality that robbery can exist before it reaches the church as well as after, for if it is retained by the individual and never given, it is nevertheless stolen.

That fact would be true of course only if the tithe, a tenth, rightly belongs to God. The supreme authority to determine the fact in the case is God Himself in His claim to it. Discussion of ownership follows in the next section of this study.

The seriousness of God's charge reveals itself in the consequences which are stated as, "Ye are cursed with a curse" (Mal. 3:9). The most crucial expression of such displeasure and penalty relates to spiritual vitality of the divine-human relationship. The prayer encounter, the communion of spirits, the trustfulness of divine providence, the confidence of acceptability, and all the wonderful aspects of one's spiritual endeavors discover food for growth in a proper relationship. Many people, however, do not experience such realities or desire them.

Therefore, more recognizable penalties come in

material forms. For the agricultural sector the loss
of crops and cattle to disease, or drought, or pests
can speak of divine actions (Mal. 3:11; Hag. 1:6-11;
and Amos 4:4-11). We face two problems of interpretation of such events: (1) concluding that every
material disaster is divine punishment and (2) concluding that any material failure is mere circum-
stance not related to divine concerns. Thus,
individuals must examine all such cases for private
learning and benefit (compare Job). But we could
do well to allow every struggle and luxury to crowd
us to Christ.

Recognition of Ownership

Recognition of one tenth of one's income as sacred began very early in history. The practice of
percentage calculations appears throughout the
nations, a universal concept, not merely Jewish.
However, sources for our study are biblical. Before
the clear statement of divine ownership in the law
given to Moses, two clear examples express love,
devotion, appreciation, and expectation. Apparently both Abram and Jacob employed a well-
known custom (Gen. 14:18-20; 28:18-22).

Clear declarative statements exist in the Mosaic
law. The definition of "tithe" as "tenth" comes in
the same passage as claim of ownership (Lev. 27:
30-32). It is the Lord's, to be set aside as special
(holy) and reserved for His use. If one accepts the

divine right to so designate that portion of our income, one can understand the corresponding responsibility of relaying it to God and conclude that not to do so is robbery. We recognize that those who do not desire divine association have greater problems than not tithing. Indeed, superficial giving would be like the vain practices of Malachi's people.

This collection of a tenth became God's method of accomplishing His ministry in a material world. The Levites who served at the tabernacle and Temple gathered provisions from the tithe (Num. 18:21-28). God provided care for "the stranger, and the fatherless, and the widow" by this method (Deut. 14:28). Thus after the time of Moses, usage was quite practical. The Jews had a tithe system which is not really clear to us. Perhaps three tithes, some annually and some triennially, amounting to 20-30 percent were collected. But of all the wrongs lodged against the Jews, forsaking the tithe was not generally a paramount practice. This use to provide ministry care explains Malachi's reference that "there may be meat in mine house" (v. 10). See also 1 Kings 7:51; Nehemiah 10:38-39; 13:12-13.

Historically, tithing appeared as official church law at the Council of Mascon in 585. In the late eighth or early ninth century, Charlemagne also made it an official state law. The Protestant groups, except Anabaptists, continued the practice. In England, tithing became a church law in 786 and a state law in AD 900. The repeal of the English tithing laws to support the state church only occurred in 1936, which explains in part why the idea found disfavor among Baptists.

Tithing and Material Prosperity—3:10-12

Four considerations aid our understanding of this topic. First, the superficial "health and wealth" theology (success) guarantees financial rewards for financial investments. Other approaches have a similar outlook assuming that serving God (money or not) always provides success in this world. It projects God like a computer which automatically tallys and returns rewards, like a slot machine or vending equipment. The approach resembles John Tetzel's peddling of indulgences which triggered specific action resulting in the Protestant Reformation. He promised that when the coin hit the cup, the troubled soul would spring from purgatory.

We need to speak not only to be understood but to avoid being misunderstood. Admittedly, this is not always possible as people interpret statements to their liking. But we must acknowledge that some tithing testimonies and sermons emphasize the material refunds to such an extent that people can easily transfer "blessings" to the physical realm.

A man in Florida sued his church because he did
not receive the "blessings, benefits, and rewards"
promised him if he gave 10 percent of his income
to the church. But a businessman in San Antonio
refunded the giver his $800 along with the follow-
ing statement: "I sympathize with anyone who
gives money to the church and sits back and expects God to immediately hand it back to him,
with interest, by some specific act. I have never
tried to make a deal with God like that, but for
thirty-six years my wife and I have found that God
will honor those who honor him."

Second, examination of some financially poor
saints of the Bible reveal that they were sincerely
devoted souls. The poor widow who gave all her
living and who was so highly complimented by
Jesus remained poor so far as we know (Luke 21:2-
3). The early Christians of the Book of Acts lived
among miracles. But the saints in Jerusalem (many
who had sold farms with great generosity) stayed
in great poverty and received relief offerings from
others (Acts 11:29-30). Joseph and Mary presented
the offering of turtle doves at Jesus' dedication
(Luke 2:23). This constituted the lowest of financial
ability of the law which granted offerings according to ability to give (Lev. 12:6-8). Challenging respect for the honestly poor, God had written,
"Hearken, my beloved breathren, Hath not God
chosen the poor of this world rich in faith, and

heirs of the kingdom which he hath promised to them that love him?" (Jas. 2:5). We conclude that with much emphasis on the poor, who are also genuinely spiritual, God does not present wealth as automatic rebate on spiritual devotion.

Third, the truly spiritual person desires and recognizes that "blessings" of the nonmaterial realm are genuine and lasting. Such people hunger to enhance the reputation of their God more than multiply their finances. They want "to do justly, and to love mercy, and to walk humbly with thy God" as a primary goal of life (Mic. 6:8). They treasure the prospect of Jesus' commendation someday to say, "Well done, thou good and faithful servant" (Matt. 25:21). They really expect heaven to afford opportunity to praise Jesus—kneel before Him while placing whatever crowns they get at His feet —rather than lord it over others who did not get as many stars or rewards as they. Such saints get the blessings of sweet communion and fellowship with God. They delight in satisfaction of having tried to serve Him dependably, of having attempted to be right, and of giving of their finances for His service in this world.

Fourth, promise of material provisions accompany consecrated living. The psalmist wrote, "I have been young, and now am old; yet have I not seen the righteous forsaken, nor his seed begging bread" (37:25). The Jerusalem saints in severe

straits would have had to interpret that statement.
Jesus urged us to avoid stressful anxiety about food
and clothes with assurance that they would be provided as God arranges for the grass and the birds
(Matt. 6:25-33). God thrust deeply into my consciousness the conviction of His provision for my
physical needs while I was in college by the thrilling discovery of Philippians 4:19. I realize that I
might have misinterpreted it, but I was sincerely
honest and trustful however limited that was. I also
accepted my responsibility of careful money man-
agement, trying to be unselfish in wants. That
verse supported me throughout the years to discover His provisions in all areas of my needs, even
beyond that original financial one. But that wonderful truth must be connected with Paul's companion statement in that chapter which described
his discipline of earthly desires as he said, "Not that
I speak in respect of want: for I have learned, in
whatsoever state I am, therewith to be content"
(Phil. 4:11). Paul did not use his resources to buy
the latest model chariot or fashioned clothes or
gourmet foods or luxurious vacation travel pack-
age. He anticipated having needs met, not wants.
Malachi 3:11 offered crop increases in response to
their obedience as does the "recipe for revival" of
2 Chronicles 7:13-14. The "windows of heaven"
probably refer to rains for the crops in both passages.

In addition to God working with us (and our working with Him) to provide our basic needs, we recognize some benefits of natural laws' operations. Wholesome living and its consequences remove some useless drain of income attendant to such conduct as gambling, drug abuse, and the like. The life-style of the prodigal son meant that he "wasted his substance with riotous living" (Luke 15:13). Some experience the high cost of low living. Another law treats financial responsibility. This practice deals with personal discipline of spending/saving/sharing. It considers wastefulness to be sinfulness.

The following conclusions merit examination. First, material prosperity fails to reveal one's spirituality. Second, God cares for His own but does not assume an automatic calculation of deed and reward accounting. Third, divine grace operates within each individual's circumstances as God remains sovereign in His choices. Fourth, the greatest rewards for devotion are in fellowship with God and in satisfaction of service. Fifth, material provisions to meet our basic needs accompany devotion.

God challenged Malachi's people to prove Him in giving abundant benefits, including crop fertility and loss protection. He required total spiritual sincerity, not merely vain giving of material tithes.

Tithing: A Divine Command—3:10

An imperative verb form for positive emphasis declares that we are to bring the full tithe into the storehouse. It is not optional nor debatable. One may discuss with the Lord His guidance to arrange the income-expense priorities. However, we need in humble, obedient love seek how we can obey, not how we can get special exemption. Christians find that the urge of gratitude and generosity underscores the tithe principle as valid beyond the command level.

Jesus warned about the personal enemy of life—selfish greed. Tithing aids one's discipline in an orderly manner. Dr. George W. Truett, famous pastor of First Baptist Church of Dallas, Texas said straightly, "A man right about this question of money is likely to be right, or easily led to do the right, on every other question of religion. A Christian man wrong on this question of his money is likely to be seriously wrong on every other question of religion. Now this is putting it strongly, but I do unhesitatingly believe every word I am saying and I would have our men lay it to heart."[2] Money is a gauge of interests. Pity the person who dreamed that God multiplied his weekly offering by ten, and that became his weekly salary.

The sincere heart might have to work at adjusting income and outgo in order to do everything one desires. A man in court for not making his support payments to his wife explained that he had to care for a mistress and eight children. Figuring the man's cigarette bill, the judge ordered him to cut down on smoking in order to pay the wife support. Christians might do well to examine their pleasure expenditures in order to find ways to tithe. Some growing Christians have budgeted a lesser percent in order to get beyond the haphazard "give when we go" plan and the irritating struggles of regular decision making of comparing bills and offerings. Genuinely, they work toward the tithe system. Churches ought to honor this noble effort and prevent multiplied demands for side offerings in Sunday School, Church Training, choir, deacons, and every unit operating separate projects. Embarrassment means that they strain to cooperate (which brings aggravation) or quit attending (which produces guilt). The side offerings cease to be "freewill."

The "storehouse" for these tithes was local in the tabernacle and the treasury of the Temple (1 Kings 7:51; Neh. 10:38-39). The support for the priests, Levites, widows, orphans, stranger, and such expenses came from tithes and other offerings (Num. 18:21; Ezra 8:25). Our society constitutes much more diversity of religious and charity organizations needing funds. A basic principle, however, concerns one's theology about the church. Since it

is indeed God's primary unit for ministering to all
peoples of the world, the church's needs for service deserve one's first allegiance with one's tithes.
The local group of saints are the only ones entrusted to the church's operation. The following account illustrates the point. A young Jewish couple
moved to California. At the appropriate season
they wanted to attend services for the High Holy
Days but were told of the $50 fee for each person
including the baby. A Rabbi later replied, "Unlike
churches that are supported by weekly collections
or tithing, synagogues are sustained by annual
membership dues. Because of the great number of
worshipers who want to attend only for the High
Holy Days, the capacity exceeds the limit, so it is
necessary to reserve seats for those who make
prior arrangements." He added that, of course,
special needs could be handled. Spiritual institu-
tions still operate in a materialistic world, and its
members should provide for its expenses. To go to
the general public with fairs, raffles, and cake sales
seems to raise questions which affect the reputation of the group. Churches might well examine
practices of the youth groups to ensure that
money-raising activities are kept within the understanding membership as they have car washes,
slave renting, and suppers.

Yahweh urged repentance of total life, including
tithing. He further challenged them to prove Him.

Apparently He expected to work with their total lives for benefit which they would recognize and enjoy.

Notes

1. Wayne Dehoney, "Tithing," Stewardship Commission, Southern Baptist Convention.

2. W. A. Criswell, *Witnessing with Our Work and Wealth*, Baptist Foundation of Texas, 1972, p. 5.

9
A New Look
at Service
Malachi 3:13 to 4:5

Have you ever questioned the value of your children? Not their worth as human biengs, but have you admitted their liability? Have you seen the freedom of friends without children against the obstacle of responsibility for children? Mother couldn't attend the conventions with all the great fellowship of friends from earlier years because of the children's schedules. Mother couldn't go on the trip to Europe because the day before departure the young son became hospitalized. Moreover, think of the economic differences. While others enjoy a cruise to exotic places, some have to use those kinds of dollars for the children's college. Does it pay to have kids?

Clarify your thinking from the limits of the above-stated reflections. Don't dwell on personal losses with blame to the children. Reflect on those nonmaterial benefits. Children come in such assorted sizes and dispositions. They can be the sweetest and hatefulest creatures rolled into one bundle. You can lock them out of your workshop but not out of your heart. You can drive them out of your study but not out of your mind. You get paid when she burst into your lap, grabs your checks between tiny hands, and says, "You're the best daddy in the whole world." You save the card on which he had scrawled, "Thanks for being a great dad." Perhaps you long for that day that people tell about when children return to childhood ideas of thinking that parents knew something or that their parents were better (tougher, smarter) than someone else's. Yes, you get paid when they achieve. At college graduation the farmer told his wife, "That's the best crop we ever raised." Yes, we get paid in nonmaterial ways for their stepping on our feet and walking on our hearts.

Similarly, have you thought about the costs of serving God? You don't fish or golf or sleep on the Lord's day because you want to study (or teach, sing, usher) and to worship. Have you noticed that others can buy sports equipment and expensive clothes on the same kind of income you have? Also, have you thought (however so briefly), "I could do that with that annual tithe amount reported on the church receipt"? Does it pay to serve Jesus?

The insulting, catty question of Malachi's complainers raised these kinds of issues. They asked, "What have we spoken so much against thee?"

Then they said that it was useless to serve God and of no profit to keep His Word and to be humble.

Misconception of Value—3:14-15

Malachi exposed their reasonings by saying, "Your words have been stout against me, saith the Lord (v. 13)." "Stout" refers to hard, harsh, or too much weight. Their pretentious innocence revealed itself in their question. The prophet proceeded to lay their evaluations in the open.

First, they discussed among themselves the worth of serving God. The evaluation culminated the previous concepts of their expectations of God and their incorrect views. The assumption appeared to be that they were sincere and devoted souls. Man's sight often reflects deception. But God's illumination must correct obscure vision.

The people considered service to Yahweh as useless, worthless, or empty (vain). Perhaps their measurement consisted of fallacies in determining what was genuine service and also what was desirable results. The prosperity of crops and of prestige did not indicate God's great reward. How are we to gauge success in God's service: size of position, recognition of fellows, or degree of easy living?

The stereotyped saint reflects a view of a dark-clothed monk isolated to his own peaceful meditation in a drab existence. Some think of the saint as a sacrificing missionary, struggling in loneliness against the rugged forces of nature, living in some shack, and recouperating from jungle diseases.

Second, the critics complained that material profit did not accrue to those who kept God's ordinances. They would not agree with the psalmists who enjoyed strength from His Word, being a light for advance in life, being tasty like honey, and being protective from infectious detriments like sin. "Profit" was a technical term for weavers cutting a piece of cloth from a loom. The critics expected such immediate payment from their work materialistically. They may not exhaust the scope of people today who consider their call and service to be underpaid.

Another aspect of the complaint centered around their mournful displays. That term reflects dark, drab clothing and practice. We are left uninformed about any degree of sincerity in this experience. We could guess that such acting was hypocritical, or at least misdirected, because of the whole context of opposition to the Lord.

Evidence for their charges opf uselessness and profitlessness arose in their comparison of status with the wicked (v. 5). Those sinners (proud, scornful) appeared blessed with happiness, set up with success, and delivered from calamity and struggles of living. Thus, God seemed to be cbnfused about whom to honor; so they lodged their strong words against Him.

Evaluation of Worth—3:16

Qualities of another group (or a part of the complainers) took a different viewpoint. Two statements classify them: "They that feared the Lord . . . and that thought upon his name." The basic element in their sight related to the person of God Himself, not His benefits. The expression "fear of the Lord" remains significant in biblical truth. It does indeed refer to a fear, fright, uneasiness. We err if we remove that basis. The experience evolves beyond fear primarily into respect of authority and reverence for Deity. Seriousness reflects an element of fear, perhaps not fright of mistreatment, but fear of displeasing a loved one. The value of disciplined attitude, which elevates God in our thinking, finds expression in "The fear of the Lord is the beginning of knowledge" (Prov. 1:7 and "wisdom" in 9:10). The term remains a virtual synonym for conscientious consecration and a holy life-style. It acknowledges His lordship authority willingly and trustfully. Consequently, those souls sense no need for correcting God in the moral governing of our world, as whether the righteous receive adequate rewards or the wicked unduly prosper.

Another facet of the righteous ones exhibits the practice of concentration upon God and His essential divine qualities. "Name" incorporated this concept within itself, reflecting one's status, nature, or character. Thus, this group thought about these aspects of their God, perhaps from Exodus 34:6-7. The sense of the verb is "to meditate," "regard," or "to focus one's mind" on something. The Greek translation (Septuagint) used the same word here as in Philippinas 4:8, "Think on these things." People's attention naturally turns toward their investments, on what they deem important, and thus reflects their real selves. "For as he thinketh in his heart, so is he" (Prov. 23:7). "For where your treasure is, there will your heart be also" (Matt. 6:21).

This involvement in spiritual evaluation can produce interesting individuals, quite contrary to the described stereotypes. The two following illustrations should aovid any misunderstanding that spiritual life guarantees material success. For these people did and would love Jesus without wealth or prestige. But we desire to realize that such earthliness does not negate true spiritual commitment. Mary Crowley weathered the loss of her mother at eighteen months of age. She also had an abusive childhood, a failed marriage, financial poverty, and two bouts with cancer. She served God while trying to make a way with two small children. Later, she married and finances no longer plagued her. But at age forty-two she sought God's guidance about beginning her own business, working in the family garage. Now, her multimillion-dollar direct-sales business operates on equal parts of biblical inspiration and personal ambition. She remembers to trust and to love God even with material success and personal prestige.

Consider the popular Tom Landry, coach of the Dallas Cowboys professional football team. He expresses quite openly his faith and commitment to Christ. Although he attended church regularly with his parents, assuming he was saved, Tom Landry became a Christian at thirty-four years of age. He went with a friend to a Bible-study breakfast and discovered what a personal relationship with Jesus really was. He considers it God's desire that he coach the Cowboys. He publicly avows to put God first, family second, and football third. He believes that serving God is vital, thus differing from Malachi's contemporaries. In the real significant areas of life, Landy expects such engagement with God to be profitable, contrary to the statements by the complainers in Malachi's day. He loves and serves the Lord because God is worthy, not for earthly rewards.

Assurance of Reward—3:17-18

Divine response offers four provisions in the text. A book of remembrance contains th- names of those who fear the Lord. Writers have described several books in Scripture. Obviously, God does not have need for records since He knows everything. But such terms reassure frail humans of God's accuracy and concern.

The covenant expression occurs in this text, "And they shall be mine." Recall Exodus 19:5 which uses this same word meaning "choice or treasured possession." The basic root of the word means "to set aside a thing or property," like drawing a ring around land to claim it as one's own. The Old Testament pictured Israel as such belonging to God in love and affection, a most prized personal possession (Deut. 7:6; 14:2; Ps. 135:4). The New Testament continued the unique relationship claim (Eph. 1:14; Titus 2:14; 1 Pet. 2:9).

Yahweh proceeded to declare His protection for these choice ones in the day of judgment. He said, "I will spare them, as a man spareth his own son that serveth him" (Mal. 3:17). In the continuing account (ch. 4), God described the punishment in vivid terms of burning stubble in an oven. Those who had asked when He would bring justice would learn it. Those who had accused Him of confused values between the righteous and the wicked would face reality.

In addition, God will care for those who trust Him with making a distinction between them and the wicked (3:18). Our limited perception may not discern between the wheat and the tares; we cannot know who really belongs to the Lord. But a part of His wonderful care is to provide and to recognize His own.

What response is appropriate from those of us who do consider God as our chief goal in life? A story comes to us about Robert E. Lee and "Stonewall" Jackson. Lee had sent a message to Jackson indicating that he would like to talk whenever it was convenient for Jackson to stop by. The message reached Jackson on a night when snow was falling heavily. He dressed and traveled by horse to General Lee's headquarters. A surprised Lee rather rebuked Jackson for facing the terrible weather for a small matter. General Jackson replied, "Sir, your slightest wish is my supreme command." Such obedience contradicts the argumentive attitude of the complainers of this text.

What value and profit accompany devoted service to God? Measurement standards differ. Many people testify that they consider that service for Jesus pays great dividends. The wages are regular —everyday. The compensation involves a sweet satisfaction of pleasing One whom you love intensely. The relationship pays every step of life's way.

Some experienced individuals have declared that time with Jesus grows sweeter, and love for Him grows stronger. Thus the genuine, permanent results of sincere services are priceless. We enjoy the rich expression of devotion in these words:

Every day with Jesus
  Is sweeter that the day before;
Every day with Jesus,
  I love Him more and more;
Jesus saves and keeps me,
  And He's the One I'm living for;
Every day with Jesus
  Is sweeter than the day before.[1]

What commitment does an evaluation of Jesus produce? Consider the words of Rhea F. Miller, set to music by George Beverly Shea, for your spiritual declaration:

I'd rather have Jesus than silver or gold,
I'd rather be His than have riches untold,
I'd rather have Jesus than houses or lands,
I'd rather be led by His nail-pierced hand
Than to be the king of a vast domain
Or be held in sin's dread sway.
I'd rather have Jesus than anything
This world affords today.[2]

Notes

1. Copyright by Percy B. Crawford. Used by Permission of Ruth Crawford Porter, owner.

2. © Copyright 1922, 1950. © Renewed 1939, 1966 by Chancel Music, Inc. Assigned to The Rodeheaver Co. (A Div. of Word, Inc.). All Rights Reserved. International Copyright Secured. Used by Permission.

Outline

Studies in the Book of Malachi

I. A New Look at Life's Situation
   A. Prophetic worth
   B. Dealing with discouragement
      1. Discouragement of being a little group
      2. Discouragement of roller-coaster response to resolution
   C. The prophet's name
   D. Environment
   E. God's Word
II. A New Look at Love—1:2 "Wherein hast thy loved us?"
   A. Love redefined
   B. Love beyond circumstances—1:2
   C. Love amidst righteousness—1:3b-4
III. A New Look at Leadership—1:6 "Wherein have we despised thy name?"
   A. Responsibility of choice
      1. Despise God—1:6
      2. Glorify God—2:2
      3. Reverence God—2:5
   B. Righteous expectations
      1. Covenant privilege (call to service)—2:5
      2. Truthfulness vs. iniquity in conduct—2:6a
      3. Private relationship vital—2:6b
   C. Responsibility of influence
      1. Purpose (lead from sin)—2:6
      2. Effect (cause of stumbling)—2:8
   D. Response
      1. Divine displeasure—1:10b
      2. Divine isolation—2:9
IV. A New Look at Worship—1:7 "Wherein have we polluted thee?"
   A. Attitude about divine worth—1:7c, 13a
   B. Expression with leftovers—1:8,12,13
   C. Contents of emptiness—1:10
   D. Expectation of divine favor—1:9-10,14

E.   Reception of Yahweh—1:11,14*b*
V.   A New Look at Marriage/Divorce—2:14 "Wherefore?"
   A.   A "lordship" matter—2:10
   B.   A mistreatment of mate—2:14*b*,16
   C.   A conscientious commitment—2:14*c*,14*d*
VI.   A New Look at Morality—2:17 "Wherein have we wearied him?"
   A.   Limited insight of God's moral evaluation—2:17*c*
   B.   Limited understanding of the scope of God's justice—2:17*d*
   C.   Corrected view of the God of justice—1:5
   D.   Corrected view of God's faithfulness—3:6
VII.   A New Look at Repentance—3:7 "Wherein shall we return?"
   A.   Identifying the real problem—3:7*c*
   B.   Facing the need for repentance—3:7*a*
   C.   Assurance in repentance—3:7*b*
VIII.   A New Look at Stewardship—3:8 "Wherein have we robbed thee?"
   A.   Tithing and the devout worshiper
   B.   Seriousness of God's charge
      1.   Robbery—3:8*a*
      2.   Curse—3:9
   C.   Recognition of worship
   D.   Tithing and material prosperity—3:10-12
      1.   Command—3:10*a*
      2.   Provisions—3:10*b*
      3.   Proof—3:10*c*
IX.   A New Look at Service—3:13 "What have we spoken so much against thee?"
   A.   Misconception of value—3:14-15
   B.   Evaluation of value—3:16
   C.   Assurance of reward—3:17-18